A SELECT GLOSSARY OF ENGLISH WORDS.

A

SELECT GLOSSARY

OF

ENGLISH WORDS USED FORMERLY IN SENSES
DIFFERENT FROM THEIR PRESENT.

BY

RICHARD CHENEVIX TRENCH, D. D.
DEAN OF WESTMINSTER,
OR OF "THE STUDY OF WORDS"—"ENGLISH, PAST AND PRESENT"—"THE
LESSONS IN PROVERBS"—"SYNONYMS OF THE NEW TESTAMENT," ETC.

REDFIELD
34 BEEKMAN STREET, NEW YORK
1859

PREFACE.

This volume is intended to be a contribution, I am aware a very slight one, to a special branch of the study of our own language. It proposes to trace in a popular manner and for general readers the changes of meaning which so many of its words have undergone; words which, as current with us as they were with our forefathers, yet mean something different on our lips from what they meant upon theirs. Of my success in carrying out the scheme which I had set before myself, it does not become me to speak, except to say that I have fallen a good deal below my hopes, and infinitely below my desires. But of the scheme itself I have no doubts. I feel sure that, if only adequately carried out, few works of the same compass could embrace matter of more manifold instruction, or in a region of knowledge which it would be more desirable to occupy. In the present condition of education in England, above all with the pressure upon young men, which is ever increasing, to complete their educational course at the earliest possible date, the number of those enjoying the inestimable advantages, mental and moral, which more than any other languages the Latin and the Greek supply, must ever be growing smaller. It becomes, therefore, a duty to seek elsewhere the best substitutes within reach for that discipline of the faculties which these languages would better than any other have afforded. And I believe, when these two are set aside, our own language and literature will furnish the best substitutes; which, even though they may not satisfy perfectly, are not, therefore, to be rejected. I am persuaded that the decomposition, word by word, of small portions of our best poetry and prose — *Lycidas* suggests itself to me as in verse offering more exactly what I seek than any other poem, perhaps some of Bacon's *Essays* in prose — the compensations which we look for are most capable of being found; even as I have little doubt that in many of our higher English schools compensations of the kind are already oftentimes obtained.

In such a decomposition, to be followed by a reconstruction, of some small portions of a great English Classic, matters almost innumerable, and pressing on the attention from every side, would claim to be noticed; but certainly not last nor least the changes which, on close examination, would be seen to have overcome many of the words employed. It is to point out some of these changes; to suggest how many more there may be, there certainly are, which have not been noticed in these pages; to show how slight and subtle, while yet most real, how easily, therefore, evading detection, unless constant vigilance is used, these changes often have been; to trace here and there the progressive steps by which the old meaning has been put off, and the new put on, the exact road which a word has travelled; this has been my purpose here; and I have desired by such means to render some small assistance to those who are disposed to regard this as a serviceable discipline in the training of their own minds or the minds of others.

The book is, as its name declares, a *Select* Glossary. There would have been no difficulty whatever in doubling or trebling the number of articles admitted into it. But my purpose being rather to arouse curiosity than fully to gratify it, to lead others themselves to take note of changes, and to account for them, rather than to take altogether this pleasant labor out of their hands and to do for them what they could more profitably do for themselves, I have consciously left much of the work undone, even as unconsciously, no doubt, I have left a great deal more. At the same time it has not been mere caprice which has induced the particular selection of words which has been actually made. Various motives, but in almost every case such as I could give account of to myself, have ruled this selection. Sometimes the past use of a word has been noted and compared with the present, as usefully exercising the mind in the tracing of minute differences and fine distinctions; or again, as helpful to the understanding of our earlier authors, and likely to deliver the readers of them from misapprehensions into which they might very easily fall; or once more, as opening out a curious chapter in the history of manners, or as involving some interesting piece of history, or some singular superstition; or again, as witnessing for the good or for the evil which have been unconsciously at work in the minds and hearts of those, who insensibly have modified in part or changed altogether the meaning of some word; or, lastly and more generally, as illustrating well under one aspect or another those permanent laws which are every where affecting and modifying human speech.

And as the words brought forward have been selected with some care, and according to certain rules which have for the most part indicated their selection, so also has it been with the passages adduced in proof of the changes of meaning which they have undergone. The principal value which a volume of such humble pretensions as the present can possess, must consist in the happiness with which these have been chosen. Not every passage, which really contains evidence of the assertion made, will for all this serve to be adduced in proof, and this I presently discovered in the many which for one cause or another it was necessary to set aside. There are various excellencies which ought to meet in such passages, but which will not by any means be found in all.

In the first place they ought to be such passages as will tell their own story, prove the point which they are cited to prove, quite independently of the uncited context, to which it will very often happen that many readers can not, and of those who can, that the larger number will not, refer. They should bear, too, upon their front, that amount of triumphant proof, which will carry conviction not merely to the student who, by a careful observation of many like passages, and a previous knowledge of what was a word's prevailing use in the time of the writer, is prepared to receive it, but to him, also, to whom all this is presented now for the first time, who has no predisposition to believe, but is disposed, rather, to be incredulous about it. Then, again, they should, if possible, be passages capable of being detached from their context without the necessity of drawing a large amount of this context after them for the making them intelligible; like trees which will endure to be transplanted without carrying with them a huge and cumbrous bulk of earth, clinging to their roots. Once more, they should, if possible, be such as have a certain intrinsic worth and value of their own, independent of their value as illustrative of the point in language directly to be proved— some weight of thought, or beauty of expression, or merit of some other kind, that so the reader may be making a second gain by the way. I can by no means claim this for all, or nearly all of mine. Indeed it would have been absurd to seek it in a book of which the aim is quite other than that of the bringing together a collection of striking quotations; any merit of this kind must continually be subordinated, and, where needful, wholly sacrificed, to the purposes more immediately in view. Still there will be many citations found in these pages which, while they fulfil the primary intention with which they were quoted, are not wanting, also, in this secondary worth.

In my citations I have throughout acted on the principle that "Enough is as good as a feast;" and that this same "Enough," as the proverb may well be completed, is better than a surfeit. So soon as that earlier meaning, from which our present is a departure, or which once subsisted side by side with our present, however it may have now disappeared, has been sufficiently established, I have held my hand, and not brought further quotations in proof. In most cases, indeed, it has seemed desirable to adduce passages from two or three authors; without which a suspicion may always remain in the mind, that we are dealing with the exceptional peculiarity of a single writer, who even in his day stood alone. I do not feel confident that in some, though rare, instances I have not brought forward exceptional uses of this kind.

Two words I will add in conclusion. Seeing that I have had some share, though a small one, in the suggestion of a new English Dictionary to be published by the Philological society, I may be permitted to say that I considered it became me to use no portion whatever of the materials which are being collected for it in the composition of this volume—of those contributions for a public object, to a private end. Indeed those materials have never so much as come under my eye, except some exceedingly small portions of them, which by accident passed through my hands on their way to those of the Editor; not to say that this little Glossary was in all essential parts completed two years ago, before that great work was so much as contemplated.

And as I owe nothing to these MS. collections, invaluable help as I have no doubt they would have rendered, so next to nothing in the way of citation to any other source. This value I may claim for my book, that it is with the very most trifling exceptions an entirely independent and original collection of passages illustrative of the history of our language. Of my citations, I believe about a thousand in all, I may owe some twenty at the most to existing Dictionaries or Glossaries, to Nares, or Johnson, or Todd, or Richardson. In perhaps some twenty cases more I have lighted upon and selected a passage by one of them selected before, and have not thought it desirable, or have not found it possible, to choose some other in its room. These excepted, the collection is entirely independent of all those which have previously been made.

WESTMINSTER, *May* 25, 1859.

SELECT GLOSSARY,

ETC.

A.

Abandon. 'Bann,' a word common to all the Germanic languages, and surviving in our '*banns* of marriage,' is open proclamation. In Low Latin it takes the forms of 'bannus,' 'bannum,' edict or interdict; while in early French we have 'bandon,' almost always with the particle *à* prefixed, 'à bandon;' thus 'vendre à bandon,' to sell by outcry. From this we have the verb 'abandonare,' which has passed into all the Romance languages; it is to proclaim, announce, but more often denounce (a bandit, 'bandetto,' is a denounced man, a proclaimed outlaw). Here is the point of contact between the present use of 'abandon' and its past. What you denounce, you loosen all the ties which bind you to it, you detach yourself from it, you forsake, in our modern sense of the word, you 'abandon' it.

Blessed shall ye be when men shall hate you, and *abandon* your name as evil [et *ejecerint* nomen vestrum tanquam malum, Vulg.] for the Son of man's sake.

Luke vi. 22. Rheims.

Beggar. Madame wife, they say that I have dreamed
And slept above some fifteen years or more.
Lady. Aye, and the time seems thirty unto me,
Being all this time *abandoned* from thy bed.

Shakespeare, *The Taming of the Shrew,* Act i. Sc. 1.

ACHIEVEMENT. I doubt whether this, the fuller form of the word, is ever used now, where 'hatchment' is intended.

As if a herald in the *atchievement* of a king, should commit the indecorum to set his helmet sideways and close; not full-faced and open, as the posture of direction and command.

Milton, *Tetrachordon.*

ADMIRE, ADMIRABLE. } It now always implies to wonder *with approval;* but was by no means restrained to this wonder *in bonam partem* of old.

Neither is it to be *admired* that Henry [the Fourth], who was a wise as well as a valiant prince . . . should be pleased to have the greatest wit of those times in his interests, and to be the trumpet of his praises.

Dryden, *Preface prefixed to the Fables.*

In man there is nothing *admirable* but his ignorance and weakness.

J. Taylor, *Dissuasive from Popery,* part ii. b. i. sect. 7.

ALCHYMY. By this we always understand now the pretended art of transmuting other metals into gold; but it was often used to express itself a certain mixed metal, which, having the appearance of gold, was yet mainly composed of brass. Thus the notion of falseness, of show and semblance not borne out by reality, frequently underlay the earlier uses of the word.

As for those gildings and paintings that were in the palace of Alcyna, though the show of it were glorious, the substance of it was dross, and nothing but *alchymy* and cosenage.

Sir J. Harrington, *A brief Allegory of Orlando Furioso.*

Whereupon out of most deep divinity it was concluded, that they should not celebrate the sacrament in glass, for the brittleness of it; nor in wood, for the sponginess of it, which would suck up the blood; nor in *alchymy*, because it was subject to rusting; nor in copper, because that would provoke vomiting; but in chalices of latten, which belike was a metal without exception.

Fuller, *The Holy War*, b. iii. c. 13.

Towards the four winds four speedy cherubim
Put to their mouths the sounding *alchemy*.

Milton, *Paradise Lost*, b. ii.

ALLOW, ALLOWANCE, ALLOWABLE. 'To allow,' from the French 'allouer,' and through it from the Latin 'allaudare,' had once a sense very often of praise or approval, which may now be said to have departed from it altogether. Thus in Cotgrave's *French and English Dictionary*, an invaluable testimony of the force and meanings which words had two centuries ago, 'allow' is rendered by 'allouer,' 'gréer,' 'approuver,' 'accepter,' and 'allowable' by 'louable.'

Mine enemy, say they, is not worthy to have gentle words or deeds, being so full of malice or frowardness. The less he is worthy, the more art thou therefore *allowed* of God, and the more art thou commended of Christ.

Homilies; Sermon against Contention.

Truly ye bear witness that ye *allow* [συνευδοκεῖτε] the deeds of your fathers.

Matt. xxiii. 28. Authorized Version.

A stirring dwarf we do *allowance* give
Before a sleeping giant.

Shakespeare, *Troilus and Cressida*, Act ii. Sc. 3.

Though I deplore your schism from the Catholic Church, yet I should bear false witness if I did not confess your decency, which I discerned at the holy duty, was very *allowable* in the consecrators and receivers.

Hacket, *The Life of Archbishop Williams*, part ii. p. 211.

AMUSE, AMUSEMENT. } The attempt which Coleridge makes to bring 'amuse' into some connection with the Muses is certainly an error; from whence we have obtained the word is harder to say. For two suggestions about it, neither of which seem to me very happy, see Diez, *Wört. d. Roman. Sprachen*, p. 236, and *Proceedings of the Philological Society*, vol. v. p. 82. Sufficient here to observe that the notion of diversion, entertainment, is comparatively of recent introduction into the word. 'To amuse' was to cause to muse, to occupy or engage, and in this sense indeed to *divert*, the thoughts and attention. The quotation from Phillips shows the word in transition to its present meaning.

Camillus set upon the Gauls, when they were *amused* in receiving their gold.

Holland, *Livy*, p. 223.

Being *amused* with grief, fear, and fright, he could not find a house in London (otherwise well known to him), whither he intended to go.

Fuller, *The Church History of Britain*, b. ix. § 44.

A siege of Maestricht or Wesel (so garrisoned and resolutely defended), might not only have *amused* but endangered the French armies.

Sir W. Temple, *Observations on the United Provinces*, c. 8.

To *amuse*, to stop or stay one with a trifling story, to make him lose his time, to feed with vain expectations, to hold in play.

Phillips, *The New World of Words.*

In a just way it is lawful to deceive the unjust enemy, but not to lie; that is, by stratagems and semblances of motions, by *amusements* and intrigues of actions, by ambushes and wit, by simulation and dissimulation.

J. Taylor, *Ductor Dubitantium*, b. iii. c. 2.

Anatomy. Now the act of dissection, but it was often used by our elder writers for the thing or object dissected, and then, as this was stripped of its flesh, for what we now call a skeleton. 'Skeleton' (*q. v.*) had then another meaning.

Here will be some need of assistants in this live, and to the quick, dissection, to deliver me from the violence of the *anatomy*.

Whitlock, *Zootomia*, p. 249.

Antiquity held too light thoughts from objects of mortality, while some drew provocatives of mirth from *anatomies*, and jugglers showed tricks with skeletons.

Sir T. Browne, *Hydriotaphia*

Animosity. While 'animosus' belongs to the best period of Latin literature, 'animositas' is of quite the later silver age. It was used in two senses; in that, first, of spiritedness or courage ('equi *animositas*,' the courage of a horse), and then, secondly, as this spiritedness in one particular direction, in that, namely, of a vigorous and active enmity or hatred (*Heb.* xi. 27. Vulg.). Of these two meanings the latter is the only one which our 'animosity' has retained; yet there was a time when it also had the other as well.

When her [the crocodile's] young be newly hatched, such as give some proof of *animosity*, audacity, and execution, those she loveth, those she cherisheth.

Holland, *Plutarch's Morals*, p. 977.

Doubtless such as are of a high-flown *animosity* affect *fortunas laciniosas*, as one calls it, a fortune that sits not strait and close to the body, but like a loose and a flowing garment.

Hacket, *The Life of Archbishop Williams*, part i. p. 30.

Cato, before he durst give the fatal stroke, spent part of the night in reading the Immortality of Plato, thereby confirming his wavering hand unto the *animosity* of that attempt.

Sir T. Browne, *Hydriotaphia*.

APPARENT, APPARENTLY. With the exception of the one phrase 'heir *apparent*,' meaning heir evident, manifest, undoubted, we do not any longer employ 'apparent' for that which appears, because it *is*, but always either for that which appears and is not, or for that which appears, leaving in doubt whether it is or no. Thus we might say with truth in the modern sense of the word, that there are *apparent* contradictions in Scripture; we could not say it in the earlier sense without denying its inspiration.

It is *apparent* foul-play; and 'tis shame
That greatness should so grossly offer it.

Shakespeare, *King John*, Act iv. Sc. 2.

The laws of God cannot without breach of Christian liberty, and the *apparent* injury of God's servants, be hid from them in a strange language, so depriving them of their best defence against Satan's temptations.

Fuller, *Twelve Sermons concerning Christ's Temptations*, p. 59.

At that time [at the resurrection of the last day], as the Scripture doth most *apparently* testify, the dead shall be restored to their own bodies, flesh and bones.

Articles of the Church (1552).

Apprehensive. As there is nothing which persons lay hold of more readily than that aspect of a subject in which it presents matter for fear, 'to apprehend' has acquired the sense of to regard with fear; yet not so as that this use has excluded its earlier; but it *has* done so in respect of 'apprehensive,' which has now no other meaning than that of fearful, a meaning once quite foreign to it.

She, being an handsome, witty, and bold maid, was both *apprehensive* of the plot, and very active to prosecute it.

Fuller, *The Profane State*, b. v. c. 5.

My father would oft speak
Your worth and virtue; and, as I did grow
More and more *apprehensive*, I did thirst
To see the man so praised.

Beaumont and Fletcher, *Philaster*, Act v. Sc. 1.

Artillery. Leaving the perplexed question of the derivation of this word, it will be sufficient to observe, that while it is now only applied to the heavy ordnance of modern warfare, in earlier use any engines for the projecting of missiles, even to the bow and arrows, would have been included under this term.

Ships heavily charged, carrying *artillery*, ordinance, and engines of battery.

Holland, *Livy*, p. 745.

So the Philistines, the better to keep the Jews thrall and in subjection, utterly bereaved them of all manner of weapon and *artillery*, and left them naked.

Jewel, *Reply to M. Harding*, Article xv.

And Jonathan gave his *artillery* unto his lad, and said unto him, Go, carry them to the city.

1 *Sam*. xx. 40. Authorized Version.

Artisan, } Artist. } Both these words have partially changed their meaning. 'Artisan' is no longer used of him who cultivates one of the *fine* arts, but those of common life. The fine arts, losing this word, have now claimed 'artist' for their exclusive property; which yet was far from belonging to them always. An 'artist' in its earlier acceptation was one who cultivated not the *fine*, but the *liberal*, arts. The classical scholar was eminently the 'artist.'

He was mightily abashed, and like an honest-minded man yielded the victory unto his adversary, saying withal, Zeuxis hath beguiled poor birds, but Parrhasius, hath deceived Zeuxis, a professed *artisan*.

Holland, *Pliny*, part ii. p. 535.

Rare *artisan*, whose pencil moves
Not our delights alone, but loves!

Waller, *Lines to Van Dyck*.

For then, the bold and coward,
The wise and fool, the *artist* and *unread*,
The hard and soft, seem all affined and kin.

Shakespeare, *Troilus and Cressida*, Act i. Sc. 3.

Nor would I dissuade any *artist* well grounded in Aristotle from perusing the most learned works any Romanist hath written in this argument. In other controversies between them and us it is dangerous, I must confess, even for well-grounded *artists* to begin with their writings, not so in this.

Jackson, *Blasphemous Positions of Jesuits*, Preface.

Some will make me the pattern of ignorance for making this Scaliger [Julius] the pattern of the general *artist*, whose own son Joseph might have been his father in many *arts*.

Fuller, *The Holy State*, b. ii. c. 8.

ASCERTAIN. Now to acquire a certain knowledge of a thing, but once to render the thing itself certain. Thus, when Swift wrote a pamphlet having this title, "A Proposal for correcting, improving, and *ascertaining* the English Tongue," he did not propose to obtain a subjective certainty of what the English language was, but to give to the language itself an objective certainty and fixedness.

Success is intended him [the wicked man] only as a curse, as the very greatest of curses, and the readiest way, by hardening him in his sin, to *ascertain* his destruction.

South, *Sermons*, vol. v. p. 286.

ASSASSINATE. Once used, by Milton at least, as is now the French 'assassiner,' the Italian 'assassinare,' in the sense of to assault treacherously and with murderous intent, even where the murderous purpose is not accomplished; and then, secondly, to extremely maltreat.

As for the custom that some parents and guardians have of forcing marriages, it will be better to say nothing of such a savage inhumanity, but only thus, that the law which gives not all freedom of divorce to any creature endued with reason, so *assassinated*, is next in cruelty.

Milton, *The Doctrine and Discipline of Divorce*, b. i. c. 12.

Such usage as your honorable lords
Afford me, *assassinated* and betrayed—

Id., *Samson Agonistes*.

ASSURE, ASSURANCE. } Both this and 'to ensure' *(q. v.)* are often used in our elder writers in the sense of to betroth or to affiance.

King Philip. Young princes, close your hands.
Austria. And your lips too; for I am well assured
That I did so, when I was first *assured*.

Shakespeare, *King John*, Act ii. Sc. 2.

I myself have seen Lollia Paulina, only when she was to go unto a wedding supper, or rather to a feast when the *assurance* was made, so beset and bedeckt all over with emeralds and pearls.

Holland, *Pliny*, part i. p. 256.

ASTONISH. 'To astonish' has now loosened itself altogether from its etymology, 'attonare' and 'attonitus.' The man 'astonished' can now be hardly said to be 'thunderstruck,' either in a literal or a figurative sense. But in several passages of *Paradise Lost* we shall quite fall below the poet's intention unless we read this meaning into the word; as no less in the prose quotation from Milton which follows.

The knaves that lay in wait behind rose up and rolled down two huge stones, whereof the one smote the king upon the head, the other *astonished* his shoulder.

Holland, *Livy*, 1124.

The cramp-fish [the torpedo] knoweth her own force and power, and being herself not benumbed, is able to *astonish* others.

Id., *Pliny*, vol. i. p. 261.

In matters of religion, blind, *astonished*, and struck with superstition as with a planet; in one word, monks.

Milton, *The History of England*, b. ii.

Astrology. As 'chemist' only little by little disengaged itself from 'alchemist,' and that, whether we have respect to the thing itself, or the name of the thing, so 'astronomer' from 'astrologer,' 'astronomy' from 'astrology.' It was long before the broad distinction between the lying art and the true science was recognized and fixed in words.

If any enchantress should come unto her, and make promise to draw down the moon from heaven, she would mock these women and laugh at their gross ignorance, who suffer themselves to be persuaded for to believe the same, as having learned somewhat in *astrology*.

Holland, *Plutarch's Morals*, p. 324.

Astronomer. See what has been said on the word preceding.

Bowe ye not to *astronomyers*, neither axe ye ony thing of fals dyvynours.

Levit. xix. 31. Wiclif.

If *astronomers* say true, every man at his birth by his constellation hath divers things and desires appointed him.

Pilkington, *Exposition upon the Prophet Aggeus*, c. i.

Atone, Atonement. The notion of satisfaction lies now in these words rather than that of reconciliation. An ‘atonement’ is the *satisfaction* of a wrong which one party has committed against another, not the *reconciliation* of two estranged parties. This last, however, was its earlier meaning; and if the word may be divided ‘at-one-ment,’ as probably it may, is in harmony with its etymology. Possibly men’s sense of the great Atonement of all, as resting on a satisfaction, may have ruled the use of the word.

> He and Aufidius can no more *atone*
> Than violentest contrarieties.
>
> Shakespeare, *Coriolanus*, Act iv. Sc. 6.

> His first essay succeeded so well, Moses would adventure on a second design, to *atone* two Israelites at variance.
>
> Fuller, *A Pisgah Sight of Palestine*, vol. ii. p. 92.

> Having more regard to their old variance than their new *attonement.*
>
> Sir T. More, *The History of King Richard III.*

> If Sir John Falstaff have committed disparagements unto you, I am of the Church, and will be glad to do my benevolence, to make *atonements* and compromises between you.
>
> Shakespeare, *The Merry Wives of Windsor*, Act i. Sc. 1.

ATTORNEY. Seldom used now except of the attorney *at law;* being one, according to Blackstone’s definition, “who is put in the place, stead, or *turn* of another to manage his matters of law;” and even in this sense it is going out of honor, and giving way to ‘solicitor.’ But formerly any who in any cause acted in the room, behalf, or turn of another, would be called his ‘attorney:’ thus Phillips (*New World of Wor*[illegible] nes attorney, “one appointed by another man to do any thing in his stead, or to take upon him the charge of his business in his absence;" and in proof of what honorable use the word might have, I need but refer to the quotation which immediately follows:—

Our everlasting and only High Bishop; our only *attorney*, only mediator, only peacemaker between God and men.

A Short Catechism, 1553.

Attornies are denied me,
And therefore *personally* I lay my claim
To my inheritance of free descent.

Shakespeare, *King Richard II.* Act ii. Sc. 3.

Tertullian seems to understand this baptism for the dead, de vicario baptismate, of baptism by an *attorney*, by a proxy, which should be baptized for me when I am dead.

Donne, *Sermons*, 1640, p. 794.

AUTHENTIC. A distinction drawn by Bishop Watson between 'genuine' and 'authentic' has been often quoted: "A *genuine* book is that which was written by the person whose name it bears as the author of it. An *authentic* book is that which relates matters of fact as they really happened." Of 'authentic' he has certainly not seized the true force, neither do the uses of it by good writers bear him out. The true opposite to αὐθεντικός in Greek is ἀδέσποτος, and 'authentic' is properly having an author, and thus coming with authority, authoritative; the connection of 'author' and 'authority' in our own language giving us the key to its successive meanings. Thus, an 'authentic' document is, in its first meaning, a document written by the proper hand of him from whom it professes to proceed. In all the passages which follow it will be observed that the word might be exchanged for 'authoritative.'

As doubted tenures, which long pleadings try,
Authentick grow by being much withstood.

Davenant, *Gondibert*, b. ii.

Which letter in the copy his lordship read over, and carried the *authentic* with him.

Hacket, *The Life of Archbishop Williams*, part ii. p. 24.

It were extreme partiality and injustice, the flat denial and overthrow of herself [*i. e.* of Justice], to put her own *authentic* sword into the hand of an unjust and wicked man.

Milton, Εἰκονοκλάστης, c. 28.

[A father] to instil the rudiments of vice into the unwary flexible years of his poor children, poisoning their tender minds with the irresistible *authentic* venom of his base example!

South, *Sermons*, vol. ii. p. 190; cf. vol. viii. p. 171.

Men ought to fly all pedantisms, and not rashly to use all words that are met with in every English writer, whether *authentic* or not.

Phillips, *The New World of Words*, Preface to 3d edit.

AWKWARD. In its present signification, unhandy, ungainly, maladroit; which yet is by no means its earlier. There is good reason to think that the same Anglo-Saxon 'aweg'* appears equally in the first syl-

* The 'awk' end of a rod is the 'away' end: thus, in Golding's *Ovid*, p. 179:—

She sprinkled us with bitter juice of uncouth herbs, and strake
The *awk* end of her charmed rod upon our heads.

Or, in the original:—

Percutimurque caput *conversæ* verbere virgæ.

lable of 'awkward' and 'wayward;' that the two words, therefore, are identical in meaning, signifying alike, *untoward*, and that, whether morally or physically, perverse, contrary, sinister, unlucky;* all earlier uses of the word bearing out this view of it.

> With *awkward* wind and with sore tempest driven
> To fall on shore.
>
> Marlowe, *Edward II.* Act iv. Sc. 6.

> The beast long struggled, as being like to prove
> An *awkward* sacrifice,† but by the horns
> The quick priest pulled him on his knees and slew him.
>
> Id., *The First Book of Lucan.*

> Was I for this nigh wrecked upon the sea,
> And twice by *awkward* wind from England's bank
> Drove back again unto my native clime?
>
> Shakespeare, 2 *Henry VI.* Act iii. Sc. 2.

> But time hath rooted out my parentage,
> And to the world and *awkward* casualties
> Bound me in servitude.
>
> *Pericles,* Act v. Sc. 1.

B.

Babe, Baby. 'Doll' is of late introduction into the English language, is certainly later than Dryden. 'Babe,' 'baby,' or 'puppet,' supplied its place.

* What makes matter, say they, if a bird sing *auke* or crow cross [si occinuerit avis]?

Holland, *Livy*, o. 247.

† Non grati victima sacri.

True religion . . . standeth not in making, setting up, painting, gilding, clothing, and decking of dumb and dead images — which be but great puppets and *babies* for old fools, in dotage and wicked idolatry, to dally and play with.

Homilies; Sermon against Peril of Idolatry.

But all as a poor pedlar did he wend,
Bearing a truss of trifles at his back,
As bells, and *babes*, and glasses, in his pack.

Spenser, *The Shepherd's Calendar, May.*

Think you that the child hath any notion of the strong contents of riper age? or can he possibly imagine there are any such delights as those his *babies* and rattles afford him?

Allestree, *Sermons*, part ii. p. 148.

Bacchanal. This would, I suppose, be used now only of the votaries of Bacchus; but it was once more accurately applied to the orgies celebrated in his honor.

They perform there certain *bacchanals* or rites in the honour of Bacchus.

Holland, *Plutarch's Morals.*

So *bacchanals* of drunken riot were kept too much in London and Westminster, which offended many, that the thanks due only to God should be paid to the devil.

Hacket, *The Life of Archbishop Williams*, part i. p. 165.

Baffle. Now to counterwork and to defeat; but once not this so much as to mock and put to shame, and, in the technical language of chivalry, it expressed a ceremony of open scorn with which a recreant or perjured knight was visited.

First he his beard did shave and foully shent,
Then from him reft his shield, and it reversed,
And blotted out his arms with falsehood blent,
And himself *baffled*, and his arms unhersed,
And broke his sword in twain, and all his armour spersed.

Spenser, *The Fairy Queen*, v. 3, 37.

He that suffers himself to be ridden, or thro' pusillanimity or sottishness will let every man *baffle* him, shall be a common laughing-stock to flout at.

Burton, *Anatomy of Melancholy*, part ii. sec. 3, mem. 7.

Alas, poor fool, how have they *baffled* thee!

Shakespeare, *Twelfth-Night*, Act v. Sc. 1.

BANQUET. At present the entire course of any solemn or splendid entertainment; but 'banquet' used generally to be restrained to the lighter and ornamental dessert or confection with wine, which followed the more substantial repast.

I durst not venture to sit *at supper* with you; should I have received you then, coming as you did with armed men to *banquet* with me? [*Convivam* me tibi committere ausus non sum; *comissatorem* te cum armatis venientem recipiam?]

Holland, *Livy*, p. 1066.

Then was the banqueting-chamber in the tilt-yard at Greenwich furnished for the entertainment of these strangers, where they did both sup and *banquet*.

Cavendish, *The Life of Cardinal Wolsey*.

We'll *dine* in the great room; but let the music
And *banquet* be prepared here.

Massinger, *The Unnatural Combat*, Act iii. Sc. 1.

BASE, BASENESS. The aristocratic tendencies of speech (tendencies illustrated by the word 'aristocracy' itself), which reappear in a thousand shapes, on the one side in such words, and their usages, as καλοκἀγαθός, ἐπιεικής, 'noble,' on the other in such as 'villain,' 'boor,' 'knave,' and in this 'base,' are well worthy of accurate observation. Thus, 'base' always now implies moral unworthiness; but did not so once. 'Base' men were no more than men of humble birth and low degree.

> But virtuous women wisely understand
> That they were born to *base* humility,
> Unless the heavens them lift to lawful sovereignty.
>
> Spenser, *The Fairy Queen*, v. 5, 25.

He that is ashamed of *base* and simple attire, will be proud of gorgeous apparel, if he may get it.

Homilies; Sermon against Excess of Apparel.

By this means we imitate the Lord Himself, who hath abased Himself to the lowest degree of *baseness* in this kind, emptying Himself (Phil. ii. 8), that He might be equal to them of greatest *baseness*.

Rogers, *Naaman the Syrian*, p. 461.

BATTLE. Once used not as now of the hostile shock of armies; but often of the army itself; or sometimes in a more special sense, of the main body of the army, as distinguished from the van and rear.

> Each *battle* sees the other's umbered face.
>
> Shakespeare, *King Henry V.* Act. iv. Chorus.

Richard led the vanguard of English; Duke Odo commanded in the main *battle* over his French; James of Auvergne brought on the Flemings and Brabanters in the rear.

Fuller, *The Holy War*, book iii. c. 11.

Where divine blessing leads up the van, and man's valour brings up the *battle*, must not victory needs follow in the rear?

Fuller, *A Pisgah Sight of Palestine*, vol. i. p. 174.

BAWD. Not confined once to one sex only, but could have been applied to pandar and pandaress alike.

He was, if I shal yeven him his laud,
A theef, and eke a sompnour and a *baud*.

Chaucer, *The Freres Tale.*

One Lamb, a notorious impostor, a fortune-teller, and an employed *bawd*.

Hacket, *The Life of Archbishop Williams*, part ii. p. 81.

A carrion crow he* is, a gaping grave,
The rich coat's moth, the court's bane, trencher's slave,
Sin's and hell's winning *bawd*, the devil's factoring knave.

P. Fletcher, *The Purple Island*, c. viii.

BEASTLY, BEASTLINESS. We translate σῶμα ψυχικόν (1 Cor. xv. 44) 'a *natural* body;' some have regretted that it was not rendered 'an *animal* body.' This is exactly what Wiclif meant when he translated the 'corpus animale' which he found in his Vulgate, 'a *beastly* body.' The word had then no ethical coloring; nor, when it first acquired such, had it exactly that which it now possesses.

It is sowen a *beestli* bodi; it shal rise a spiritual bodi.

1 *Cor*. xv. 44. Wiclif.

Where they should have made head with the whole army upon the Parthians, they sent him aid by small companies; and when they

* The flatterer.

were slain, they sent him others also. So that by their *beastliness* and lack of consideration they had like to have made all the army fly.

North, *Plutarch's Lives*, p. 769.

BLACKGUARD. The scullions and other meaner retainers in a great household, who, when progress was made from one residence to another, accompanied and protected the pots, pans, and other kitchen utensils, riding among them and being smutted by them, were contemptuously styled the 'black guard.' It is easy to trace the subsequent history of the word. With a slight forgetfulness of its origin, he is now called a 'blackguard,' who would have been once said to belong to the 'black guard.'

Close unto the front of the chariot marcheth all the sort of weavers and embroderers; next unto whom goeth the *black guard* and kitchenry.

Holland, *Ammianus*, p. 12.

A lousy slave, that within this twenty years rode with the *black guard* in the Duke's carriage, mongst spits and dripping-pans.

Webster, *The White Devil.*

Thieves and murderers took upon them the cross to escape the gallows; adulterers did penance in their armour. A lamentable case that the Devil's *black guard* should be God's soldiers!

Fuller, *The Holy War*, b. i. c. 12.

Dukes, earls, and lords, great commanders in war, common soldiers and kitchin boys were glad to trudge it on foot in the mire hand in hand, a duke or earl not disdaining to support or help up one of the *black guard* ready to fall, lest he himself might fall into the mire, and have none to help him.

Jackson, *A Treatise of the Divine Essence and Attributes*, b. vi. c. 28.

Bleak. It is not often that 'bleak' (=the German 'bleich,' pale, white) comes out so clearly in its original identity with 'bleach' as in the following quotation. I do not myself remember to have met another passage of the kind.

When she came out, she looked as pale and as *bleak* as one that were laid out dead.

Foxe, *The Book of Martyrs; the Escape of Agnes Wardall.*

Bombast. Now inflated diction, words which, sounding lofty and big, have no real substance about them. This, which is now the sole meaning, was once only the secondary and the figurative, 'bombast' being literally the cotton wadding with which garments are stuffed out and lined, and often so used by our writers of the Elizabethan period, and then by a vigorous image transferred to what now it exclusively means.

Certain I am there was never any kind of apparel ever invented, that could more disproportion the body of man than these doublets, stuffed with four, five, or six pound of *bombast* at the least.

Stubs, *The Anatomy of Abuses*, p. 23.

The foresaid merchants transport thither ermines and grey furs, with other rich and costly skins; others carry clothes made of cotton or *bombast.*

Hackluyt, *Voyages*, vol. i. p. 93.

Bombast, the cotton-plant growing in Asia.

Phillips, *The New World of Words.*

Boot. I do not know the history of the word 'boot' as describing one part of a carriage; but it is plain that not the luggage, but the chief persons, used once to ride in the 'boot.'

His coach being come, he causeth him to be laid in softly, and so he in one *boot*, and the two chirurgeons in the other, they drive away to the very next country house.

Reynolds, *God's Revenge against Murther*, b. i. hist. 1.

He [James the First] received his son into the coach, and found a slight errand to leave Buckingham behind, as he was putting his foot in the *boot*.

Hacket, *The Life of Archbishop Williams*, part i. p. 196.

Bounty. The tendency to accept freedom of giving in lieu of all other virtues, or at least to regard it as the chiefest of all, the same which has brought 'charity' to be for many identical with almsgiving, displays itself in our present use of 'bounty,' which, like the French 'bonté,' meant goodness once.

For tho the peple have no gret insight
In virtue, he considered ful right
Hire *bountee*, and disposed that he wold
Wedde hire only, if ever he wedden shold.

Chaucer, *The Clerkes Tale.*

Nourishing meats and drinks in a sick body do lose their *bounty*, and augmenteth malady.

Sir T. Elyot, *The Governor*, b. ii. c. 7.

Brat, the same word as 'brood,' is now used always in contempt, but was not so once.

O Israel, O household of the Lord,
O Abraham's *brats*, O brood of blessed seed,
O chosen sheep, that loved the Lord indeed.

Gascoigne, *De Profundis.*

Take heed how thou layest the bane for the rats,
For poisoning thy servant, thyself, and thy *brats*.

Tusser, *Points of Good Husbandry*.

BRAVE, BRAVERY. } The derivation of 'brave' is altogether uncertain (Diez, p. 67); we obtained it in the sixteenth century, the Germans in the seventeenth (Grimm [*s. v.* 'brav'] says during the Thirty Years' War), from one or other of the Romance languages. I do not very clearly trace by what steps it obtained the meaning of showy, gaudy, rich, which once it so frequently had, in addition to that meaning which it still retains.

His clothes [St. Augustine's] were neither *brave*, nor base, but comely.

Fuller, *The Holy State*, b. iv. c. 10.

If he [the good yeoman] chance to appear in clothes above his rank, it is to grace some great man with his service, and then he blusheth at his own *bravery*.

Id., *Ib.* b. ii. c. 18.

Man is a noble animal, splendid in ashes, and pompous in the grave, solemnizing nativities and deaths with equal lustre, not omitting ceremonies of *bravery* in the infamy of his nature.

Sir T. Browne, *Hydriotaphia*.

There is a great festival now drawing on, a festival designed chiefly for the acts of a joyful piety, but generally made only an occasion of *bravery*.

South, *Sermons*, vol. ii. p. 285.

BRITAIN, BRITANY. } The distinction between these is perfectly established now: by the first we always intend *Great* Britain; by the second, the French duchy, corresponding to the ancient Armorica. But it was long before this usage was accurately settled and accepted by all. By 'Britany' Great Britain was frequently intended, and *vice versâ*. Thus, in each of the passages which follow, the other word than that which actually is used would be now employed.

> He [Henry VII.] was not so averse from a war, but that he was resolved to choose it, rather than to have *Britain* carried by France, being so great and opulent a duchy, and situate so opportunely to annoy England, either for coast or trade.
>
> Bacon, *History of King Henry VII.*

> The letter of Quintus Cicero, which he wrote in answer to that of his brother Marcus, desiring of him an account of *Britany*.
>
> Sir T. Browne, *Musæum Clausum.*

> And is it this, alas! which we
> (O irony of words!) do call *Great Britany?*
>
> Cowley, *The Extasy.*

Bullion. Now uncoined, unstamped gold or silver, but with no intimation in the word that it is of a lower standard than that which has passed through the Mint. It is otherwise, as is well known, with the French 'billon,' which is "toute matière d'or ou d'argent décriée, et qui se trouve à plus bas titre que celui d'ordonnance." It was otherwise also once with our own 'bullion.' The globular hollow buttons now retained only on the dress of pages, but formerly an ornament of gallants, and which certainly would not have been, even then, of any very precious metal, were also called bullions; it is just possible that a recollection of 'bulla,' a bubble, may have coöperated here.

> In his French doublet with his blistered *bullions.*
>
> Beaumont and Fletcher, *The Beggars' Bush,* Act iv. Sc. 4.

> Words, whilom flourishing,
> Pass now no more, but, banished from the court,
> Dwell with disgrace among the vulgar sort;
> And those which eld's strict doom did disallow,
> And damn for *bullion,* go for current now.
>
> Sylvester, *Divine Weeks of Du Bartas, Babylon.*

Buxom. The modern spelling of 'buxom' (it was somewhat, though not much better, when it was spelt 'bucksome') has quite hidden its identity with the German 'biegsam,' 'beugsam,' bendable, pliable, and so obedient. Ignorant of the history of the word, and trusting to the feeling and impression which it conveyed to their minds, men spoke of '*buxom* health' and the like, meaning by this, having a cheerful comeliness. The epithet in this application is Gray's, and Johnson justly finds fau. with it. Milton, when he joins 'buxom' with 'blithe and debonair,' and Crashaw, in his otherwise beautiful line—

> "I am born
> Again a fresh child of the *buxom* morn"—

show that already for them the true meaning of the word, common enough in our earlier writers, had passed away.

I submit myself unto this holy Church of Christ, to be ever *buxom* and obedient to the ordinance of it, after my knowledge and power, by the help of God.

Foxe, *Book of Martyrs; Examination of William Thorpe.*

Buxom, kind, tractable, and pliable one to the other.

Holland, *Plutarch's Morals*, p. 316.

[Love] tyrannizeth in the bitter smarts
Of them that to him *buxom* are and prone.

Spenser, *The Fairy Queen*, iii. 2, 23.

BY AND BY. Now a future more or less remote from the actual present; but when our Version of the Bible was made, the nearest possible future. The inveterate procrastination of men has put 'by and by' farther and farther off. Already in Barrow's time it had acquired its present meaning.

And some counselled the Archbishop to burn me *by and by*, and some other counselled him to drown me in the sea, for it is near hand there.

Foxe, *Book of Martyrs; Examination of William Thorpe.*

Give me *by and by* [ἐξαυτῆς] in a charger the head of John the Baptist.

Mark vi. 25. Authorized Version.

These things must first come to pass; but the end is not *by and by* [εὐθέως].

Luke xxi. 9. Authorized Version.

When Demophantus fell to the ground, his soldiers fled *by and by* [εὐθὺς ἔφυγον] upon it.

North, *Plutarch's Lives*, p. 308.

C.

Caitiff. The same word as 'captive;' the only difference being that 'captive' is derived directly from the Latin 'caitiff,' through the interposition of the Norman-French; it had once the same meaning with it. The deep-felt conviction of men that slavery breaks down the moral character, a chief argument against it, but unhappily also a chief difficulty in removing it, this, so grandly unfolded by Horace (*Carm.* iii. 5), and speaking out in the Italian 'cattivo,' in the French 'chétif,' speaks out with no less distinctness in the change of meaning which 'caitiff' has undergone, signifying, as it now does, one of a base, abject disposition, while there was a time when it had nothing of this in it.

Aristark, myne evene *caytyf* [concaptivus meus, Vulg.], greetith you wel.

Col. iv. 10. Wiclif.

The riche Crœsus, *caitif* in servage.

Chaucer, *The Knightes Tale.*

Avarice doth tyrannize over her *caitife* and slave, not suffering him to use what she commanded him to win

Holland, *Plutarch's Morals*, p. 208.

Capitulate. There is no reason why the reducing of any agreement to certain heads or 'capitula' should not be called 'to capitulate,' the victor thus 'capitulating' as well as the vanquished; and the present limitation of the word's use, by which it means to surrender on certain specified terms, is quite of modern introduction.

Gelon the tyrant, after he had defeated the Carthaginians near to the city Himera, when he made peace with them, *capitulated*, among other articles of treaty, that they should no more sacrifice any infants to Saturn.

Holland, *Plutarch's Morals*, p. 405.

He [the Emperor Charles V.] makes a voyage into England, and there *capitulates* with the King, among other things, to take to wife his daughter Mary.

Heylin, *History of the Reformation.*

CARPET. The covering only of floors at present, but once of tables as well.

In the fray one of their spurs engaged into a *carpet* upon which stood a very fair looking-glass and two noble pieces of porcelain, drew all to the ground, broke the glass.

Harleian Miscellany, vol. x. p. 189.

Private men's halls were hung with altar-cloths; their *tables* and beds covered with copes, instead of *carpets* and coverlets.

Fuller, *The Church History of Britain*, b. vii. § 2, 1.

CARRIAGE. Now, that which carries, or the act of carrying; but once, that which was carried, and thus baggage. From ignorance of this, the Authorized Translation, at Acts xvii. 22, has been often found fault with, but unjustly.

Spartacus charged his [Lentulus'] lieutenants that led the army, gave them battle, overthrew them, and took all their *carriage* [τὴν ἀποσκευὴν ἅπασαν].

North, *Plutarch's Lives*, p. 470.

And David left his *carriage* [τὰ σκεύη αὐτοῦ, LXX., rightly] in the hand of the keeper of the *carriage*.

1 *Sam.* xvii. 22. Authorized Version.

CATTLE. This and 'chattel' are only different forms of the same word. At a time when wealth mainly consisted in the number of *heads* of cattle *(capita, capitalia)*, the word which designated *them* easily came to signify all other kinds of property as well. (Note the well-known parallel in 'pecus,' and 'pecunia,' and in the fact that our English 'fee' is the German 'Vieh.') At a later day this was found to have its inconveniences; which some of the writers of the Elizabethan age sought to remedy by using the term '*quick* cattle,' when they intended live stock; so Sir J. Harrington *(Epigrams*, i. 91), and Puttenham *(Art of English Poesy*, b. i. c. 18). The distinction, however, was more effectually asserted by the appropriating of the several forms 'cattle' and 'chattel,' one to the living, the other to the dead.

A womman that hadde a flux of blood twelve yeer, and hadde spendid all hir *catel* [omnem *substantiam* suam, Vulg.] in leechis.

Luke viii. 43, 44. Wiclif.

The avaricious man hath more hope in his *catel* than in Jesu Christ.

Chaucer, *The Persones Tale.*

CENSURE. It does not speak well for the charity of men's judgments, that 'censure,' which designated once favorable and unfavorable judgments alike, is now restricted to unfavorable; for it must be that the latter, being by far the most frequent, have in this way appropriated the word exclusively to themselves.

His [Richard, Earl of Cornwall's] voyage was variously *censured;* the Templars, who consented not to the peace, flouted thereat, as if all this while he had laboured about a difficult nothing; others thought he had abundantly satisfied any rational expectation.

Fuller, *The Holy War*, b. iv. c. 8.

—Which could not be past over without this *censure;* for it is an ill thrift to be parsimonious in the praise of that which is very good.

Hacket, *The Life of Archbishop Williams*, part ii. p. 13.

CHAFFER. Once, to buy, to make a bargain, to higgle or dispute about the making of a bargain, it has at length seen the buying or bargaining quite disappear from it; so that 'to chaffer' is now to talk much and idly.

That no man overgo, nether disceyve his brother in *chaffaringe* [in negotio, Vulg.].

1 *Thess.* iv. 6. Wiclif.

He comaundid his servauntis to be clepid, to whiche he hadde geve money: to witte how myche ech had wonne by *chaffarynge*.

Luke xix. 15. Wiclif.

Where is the fair flock thou was wont to lead?
Or been they *chaffred*, or at mischief dead?

Spenser, *The Shepherd's Calendar*, Ecl. 9.

CHAOS. The earliest meaning of χάος in Greek, of 'chaos' in Latin, was, empty infinite space, the *yawning* kingdom of darkness; only a secondary, that which we have now adopted, namely, the rude, confused, inorganized matter out of which the universe according to the heathen cosmogony was formed. But there are evidences that the primary use of 'chaos' was not strange to the literature of the sixteenth century.

> Beside all these things, between us and you there is fixed a great *chaos*, that they which will pass from hence to you, may not.
>
> *Luke*, xvi. 26. Rheims.

> And look what other thing soever besides cometh within the *chaos* of this monster's mouth, be it beast, boat, or stone, down it goeth incontinently that foul great swallow of his.
>
> Holland, *Plutarch's Morals*, p. 975.

Cheer. Cicero, who loves to bring out superiorities, where he can find them, of the Latin language over the Greek, urges this as one, that the Greek has no equivalent to the Latin 'vultus' (*Leg*. i. 9, 27); the countenance, that is, as the ever-varying exponent of the sentiments and passions of the soul. Perhaps it may be charged on the English, that it too is now without such a word. But 'cheer,' in its earlier uses, of which certain vestiges still survive, was exactly such.

> In swoot of thi *cheer* thou schalt ete thi breed, till thou turne ayen in to the erthe of which thou art takun.
>
> *Gen*. iii. 19. Wiclif.

> And Cayn was wrooth greetli, and his *cheer* felde doun.
>
> *Gen*. iv. 5. Wiclif.

> Each froward threatening *cheer* of fortune makes us plain;
> And every pleasant show revives our woful hearts again.
>
> Surrey, *Ecclesiastes*, c. 3.

CHEMIST, CHEMISTRY. The distinction between the alchemist and the chemist, that the first is the dreamer, the insane searcher after the philosopher's stone or the elixir vitæ, the other the follower of a true and scientific method in a particular region of nature, is of comparatively recent introduction into the language. 'Chemist' is = 'alchemist' in the quotations which follow.

Five sorts of persons he [Sir Edward Coke] used to foredesign to misery and poverty; *chemists*, monopolizers, concelers, promoters, and rythming poets.

Fuller, *The Worthies of England*, *Norfolk*.

I have observed generally of *chymists* and theosophists, as of several other men more palpably mad, that their thoughts are carried much to astrology.

H. More, *A brief Discourse of Enthusiasm*, sect. 45.

Hence the fool's paradise, the statesman's scheme,
The air-built castle, and the golden dream,
The maid's romantic wish, the *chemist's* flame,
The poet's vision of eternal fame.

Pope, *The Dunciad*, b. iii. 9–12.

He that follows *chemistry* must have riches to throw away upon the study of it; whatever he gets by it, those furnaces must be fed with gold.

South, *Sermons*, vol. ix. p. 277.

CHEST. I am not aware that 'cista' was ever used in the sense of a coffin, but 'chest' is continually so used in our early English; and 'to chest,' for to place in a coffin, occurs in the heading of a chapter in our Bibles, *Gen.* l. 26: "He [Joseph] dieth, and is *chested*."

He is now ded, and nailed in his *cheste*.
Chaucer, *The Clerkes Prologue.*

Your body is now wrapt in *chest*,
I pray to God to give your soul good rest.
Hawes, *The Pastime of Pleasure*, cap. 14.

CHIMNEY. This, which means now the gorge or vent of a furnace or fire, was once used often for the furnace itself; in this more true to its origin; being derived from the Greek κάμινος, as it passed into the Latin 'caminus,' and the French 'cheminée.' The fact that it is the 'chimney,' in the modern use of the word, which, creating a draught, alone gives fierceness or activity to the flame, probably explains the present limitation of the meaning of the word. In Scotland, 'chimney' still is, or lately was, "the grate or iron frame that holds the fire" (*Scoticisms*, Edinburgh, 1787).

And his feet [were] like to latoun as in a brennynge *chymeney*.
Rev. i. 15. Wiclif.

The Son of Man shall send his angels, and shall gather all hindrances out of his kingdom and all that worketh unlawfulness, and shall cast them into the *chimney* of fire.
Matt. xiii. 50. Sir John Cheke.

CHIVALRY. It is a striking evidence of the extent to which in the feudal times the men-at-arms, the mounted knights, were esteemed as the army, while the footmen were regarded as little better than a supernumerary rabble—another record of this contempt probably surviving in the word 'infantry'—that 'chivalry,' which of course is but a different form of 'cavalry,' could once be used as convertible with army. It needed more than one Agincourt to teach that this was so no longer.

Abymalach forsothe aroos, and Phicol, the prince of his *chyvalrye* [princeps *exercitûs* ejus, Vulg.], and turneden ayen into the loond of Palestynes.

Gen. xxi. 33. Wiclif.

CHRISTEN, CHRISTENDOM. By 'Christendom' we now understand that portion of the world which makes profession of the faith of Christ, as contradistinguished from all heathen and Mahomedan lands. But it was often used by our early writers as itself the profession of Christ's faith, or sometimes for baptism, inasmuch as in that this profession was made; which is also the explanation of the use of 'christen' as equivalent to 'christianize' below. In Shakespeare our present use of 'Christendom' very much predominates, but once or twice he uses it in its earlier sense, as do authors much later than he.

Most part of England in the reign of King Ethelbert was *christened*, Kent only excepted, which remained long after in misbelief and *unchristened.*

E. K., *Gloss. to Spenser's Shepherd's Calendar, September.*

Sothli we ben togidere biried with him bi *christendom* [per baptismum, Vulg.] in to death.

Rom. vi. 4. Wiclif.

By my *christendom*,
So I were out of prison and kept sheep,
I should be merry as the day is long.

Shakespeare, *King John*, Act iv. Sc. 1.

They all do come to him with friendly face,
When of his *christendom* they understand.
Sir J. Harrington, *Orlando Furioso*, b. xliii. c. 189.

The draughts of intemperance would wash off the water of my *christendom;* every unclean lust does as it were bemire and wipe out my contract with my Lord.
Allestree, *Sermons*, vol. ii. p. 161.

CHURCH. It is in general accounted a pure oversight on the part of our Translators that they have allowed "robbers of *churches*" to remain at *Acts* xix. 37, as the rendering of ἱεροσύλους, sounding, as it does, like an anachronism on the lips of the town-clerk of Ephesus. Doubtless "spoilers of *temples*," or some such phrase, would have been preferable; yet was there not any oversight here. The title of 'church,' which we with a fit reverence restrain to a Christian place of worship, was in earlier English not refused to the Jewish, or, as in that place, even to a heathen, temple.

And, lo, the veil of the *church* was torn in two parts from the top downwards.
Matt. xxvii. 51. Sir John Cheke.

To all the gods devoutly she did offer frankincense,
But most above them all the *church* of Juno she did cense.
Golding, *Ovid's Metamorphosis*, b. xi.

These troops should soon pull down the *church* of Jove.
Marlowe, *The First Book of Lucan.*

CIVIL, CIVILITY. The tendency which there is in the meaning of words to run to the surface, till they lose and leave behind all their deeper significance, is well exemplified in the words 'civil' and 'civility'—words of how deep an import once, how slight and shallow now! A *civil* man now is one observant of slight external courtesies in the mutual intercourse between man and man; a *civil* man once was one who fulfilled all the duties and obligations flowing from his position as a 'civis,' and his relations to the other members of that 'civitas' to which he belonged, and 'civility' the condition in which those were recognized and observed. The gradual departure of all deeper significance from the word 'civility' has obliged the creation of another word, 'civilization,' which only came up toward the conclusion of the last century. Johnson does not know it in his Dictionary, except as a technical legal term to express the turning of a criminal process into a civil one; and, according to Boswell, altogether disallowed it in the sense which it has now acquired.

That wise and *civil* Roman, Julius Agricola, preferred the natural wits of Britain before the laboured studies of the French.

Milton, *Areopagitica.*

As for the Scythian wandering Nomades, temples sorted not with their condition, as wanting both *civility* and settledness.

Fuller, *The Holy State,* b. iii. c. 24.

Then were the Roman fashions imitated and the gown; after a while the incitements also and materials of vice and voluptuous life, proud buildings, baths, and the elegance of banquetings; which the foolisher sort called *civility,* but was indeed a secret art to prepare them for bondage.

Milton, *The History of England,* b. ii.

Let us remember also that *civility* and fair customs were but in a narrow circle till the Greeks and Romans beat the world into better manners.

J. Taylor, *Ductor Dubitantium*, b. ii. c. 1, § 19.

The last step in this [spiritual] death is the death of *civility*. *Civil* men come nearer the saints of God than others, they come within a step or two of heaven, and yet are shut out.

Preston, *Description of Spiritual Death and Life*, 1636, p. 59.

CLERGY. The use of 'clergy' in the abstract for learning or for a learned profession, is, it needs hardly be said, the result of the same conditions which made 'clerk' equivalent to scholar.

Was not Aristotle, for all his *clergy*,
For a woman wrapt in love so marvellously,
That all his cunning he had soon forgotten?

Hawes, *The Pastime of Pleasure.*

Also that every of the said landlords put their second sons to learn some *clergy*, or some craft, whereby they may live honestly.

State Papers, State of Ireland, 1515, vol. ii. p. 30.

CLUMSY. A word about which little satisfactory has as yet found its way into our dictionaries; but although of no very frequent use in our early literature (it does not once occur in Shakespeare), neither can it be said to be very rare; and where it occurs, it is in a sense going before its present, namely, in that of stiff, rigid, *clumped* and contracted with cold. It is familiar to all how 'clumsy,' in our modern use of the word, the fingers are when in this condition, and thus it is easy to trace the growing of the modern meaning out of the old. There are some observations on the probable etymology of the word in the *Proceedings of the Philological Society*, vol. v. p. 146.

> *Rigido;* Stark, stiffe, or num through cold, *clumzie.*
>
> Florio, *New World of Words.*

> *Havi de froid;* Stiffe, *clumpse,* benummed.
>
> Cotgrave, *A French and English Dictionary.*

> The Carthaginians followed the enemies in chase as far as Trebia, and there gave over; and returned into the camp so *clumsy* and frozen [et ita *torpentes gelu* in castra rediere] as scarcely they felt the joy of their victory.
>
> Holland, *Livy,* p. 425.

> This bloom of budding beauty loves not to be handled by such nummed and so *clomsie* hands.
>
> Florio, *Montaign's Essays,* b, iii. c. 5.

CLIMATE. At present the temperature of a region, but once the region itself—the region, however, contemplated in its slope or inclination from the equator toward the pole, and therefore, by involved consequence, in respect of its temperature; which circumstance is the point of contact between the present meaning of 'climate' and the past. We have derived the word from the mathematical geographers of antiquity. They were wont to run imaginary parallel lines, or such at least as they intended should be parallel, to the equator; and the successive 'climates' (κλίματα) of the earth were the spaces and regions between these lines.

> When these prodigies
> Do so conjointly meet, let not men say,

"These are their causes — they are natural;"
For, I believe, they are portentous things
Unto the *climate* that they point upon.

Shakespeare, *Julius Cæsar*, Act. i. Sc. 3.

This *climate* of Gaul [hanc Galliarum *plagam*] is enclosed on every side with fences that environ it naturally.

Holland, *Ammianus*, p. 47.

Climate, a portion of the earth contained between two circles parallel to the equator.

Phillips, *The New World of Words.*

COMFORT, COMFORTABLE. The verb 'confortare,' not found in classical Latin, but so frequent in the Vulgate, is first, as is plain from the 'fortis' which it embodies, to make strong, to corroborate, and only in a secondary sense, to console. We often find it in our early literature employed in that its proper sense.

And the child wexed, and was *counfortid* [confortabatur, Vulg.] in spirit.

Luke i. 80. Wiclif.

And there appeared an angel unto Him from heaven, *comforting* Him [ἐνισχύων αὐτόν].

Luke xxii. 43. Tyndale.

Thy conceit is nearer death than thy powers; for my sake, be *comfortable;* hold death awhile at the arm's end.

Shakespeare, *As you like it*, Act ii. Sc. 6.

COMMON-SENSE. The manner is very curious in which the metaphysical or theological speculations, to which the busy world was indifferent, or from which it was entirely averse, do yet in their results descend to it, and are adopted by it; while it remains quite unconscious of the source from which they spring, and counts that it has created them for itself and out of its own resources. Thus, probably most persons would almost wonder if asked the parentage of this phrase, 'common-sense,' would count it the most natural thing in the world that such a phrase should have been formed, that it demanded no ingenuity to form it, that the uses to which it is now put are the same which it has served from the first. Indeed, neither Reid, Beattie, nor Stewart, seem to have assumed anything else. But in truth this phrase, 'common-sense,' meant once something very different from that plain wisdom, the common heritage of men, which now we call by this name, having been bequeathed to us by a very complex theory of the senses, and of a *sense* which was the *common* bond of them all, and which passed its verdicts on the reports which they severally made to it. This theory of a κοινὸς νοῦς, familiar to the Greek metaphysicians, is sufficiently explained by the interesting quotation from Henry More. In Hawes' *Pastime of Pleasure* (cap. 24) the relation between the 'common wit' and the 'five wits' is at large set forth.

But for fear to exceed the commission of an historian (who with the outward senses may only bring in the species, and barely relate facts, not with the *common sense* pass verdict or censure on them), I would say they had better have built in some other place, especially having room enough besides, and left this floor, where the Temple stood, alone in her desolations.

Fuller, *The Holy War*, b. i. c. 4.

That there is some particular or restrained seat of the *common sense* is an opinion that even all philosophers and physicians are agreed upon. And it is an ordinary comparison amongst them, that the external senses and the *common sense* considered together are like a circle with five lines drawn from the circumference to the centre. Wherefore, as it has been obvious for them to find out particular organs for the external senses, so they have also attempted to assign some distinct part of the body to be an organ of the *common sense;* that is to say, as they discovered sight to be seated in the eye, hearing in the ear, smelling in the nose, &c., so they conceived that there is some part of the body wherein seeing, hearing, and all other perceptions meet together, as the lines of a circle in the centre, and that there the soul does also judge and discern of the difference of the objects of the outward senses.

H. More, *Immortality of the Soul,* b. iii. c. 13.

COMPANION. "The term 'companion' was formerly used contemptuously, in the same way in which we still use its synonyme 'fellow.' The notion originally involved in companionship, or accompaniment, would appear to have been rather that of inferiority than of equality. A companion (or *comes)* was an attendant." Craik, *English of Shakespeare*, p. 255.

I scorn you, scurvy *companion.*

Shakespeare, 2 *Henry IV.* ii. 4.

The young ladies, who thought themselves too much concerned to contain themselves any longer, set up their throats all together against my protector. "Scurvy *companion!* saucy tarpaulin! rude, impertinent fellow! did he think to prescribe to grandpapa!"

Smollett, *Roderick Random,* vol. i. c. 3.

CONCEITED, CONCEITEDLY. 'Conceit' is so entirely and irrecoverably lost to the language of philosophy, that it would be well if 'concept,' used often by our earlier philosophical writers, were revived. Yet 'conceit' has not so totally forsaken all its former meanings (for there are still '*happy* conceits' in poetry), as have 'conceited,' which once meant well conceived, and 'conceitedly.'

> Oft did she heave her napkin to her eyne,
> Which had on it *conceited* characters.
>
> Shakespeare, *A Lover's Complaint.*

> Triumphal arches the glad town doth raise,
> And tilts and tourneys are performed at court,
> *Conceited* masques, rich banquets, witty plays.
>
> Drayton, *The Miseries of Queen Margaret.*

> Cicero most pleasantly and *conceitedly.*
>
> Holland, *Suetonius*, p. 21.

CONCUBINE. No notice is taken in our dictionaries that the male paramour as well as the female was sometimes called by this name; on the contrary, their definitions exclude this.

> The Lady Anne did falsely and traiterously procure divers of the King's daily and familiar servants to be her adulterers and *concubines.*
>
> *Indictment of Anne Boleyn.*

COPY. A more Latin use of 'copy,' as 'copia' or abundance, was at one time frequent in English. It is easy to trace the steps by which the word attained its present significance. The only way to obtain 'copy' (in this Latin sense) or abundance of any document, would be by taking 'copies' (in our present sense) of it.

We cannot follow a better pattern for elocution than God Himself. Therefore He, using divers words in his Holy Writ, and indifferently for one thing in nature, we may use the same liberty in our English versions out of Hebrew or Greek, for that *copy* or store that He hath given us.

The Translators [*of the Bible,* 1611] *to the Reader.*

Drayton's heroical epistles are well worth the reading also, for the purpose of our subject, which is to furnish an English historian with choice and *copy* of tongue.

Bolton, *Hypercritica,* p. 235.

CORPSE. Now only used for the body abandoned by the spirit of life, but once for the body of the living man equally as of the dead; now only = 'cadaver,' but once 'corpus' as well.

A valiant *corpse,* where force and beauty met.

Surrey, *On the Death of Sir T. Wyatt.*

But naked, without needful vestiments
To clad his *corpse* with meet habiliments,
He cared not for dint of sword or spear.

Spenser, *The Fairy Queen,* b. vi. c. 4.

Your conjuring, cozening, and your dozen of trades
Could not relieve your *corps* with so much linen
Would make you tinder, but to see a fire.

Ben Jonson, *The Alchemist,* Act i. Sc. 1.

COURTESAN. The Low Latin 'cortesanus' was once one haunting the court, a courtier, 'aulicus,' though already in Shakespeare we often meet the present application of the word.

By the wolf, no doubt, was meant the Pope, but the fox was resembled to the prelates, *courtesans*, priests, and the rest of the spirituality.

Foxe, *The Book of Martyrs*, ed. 1641, vol. i. p. 511.

CUNNING. The fact that so many words implying knowledge, art, skill, obtain in course of time a secondary meaning of crooked knowledge, art which has degenerated into artifice, skill used only to circumvent, which meanings partially or altogether put out of use their primary, is a mournful witness to the way in which intellectual gifts are too commonly misapplied. Thus, there was a time when the Latin 'dolus' required the epithet 'malus,' as often as it signified a treacherous or fraudful device; but it was soon able to drop this as superfluous, and to stand by itself. Other words which have gone the same downward course are the following: τέχνη, 'astutia,' 'calliditas,' 'List,' 'Kunst,' and our English 'cunning'—the last, indeed, as early as Lord Bacon, who says, "We take *cunning* for a sinister or crooked wisdom," had acquired what is now its only acceptation; but not then, nor till long after, to the exclusion of its more honorable use. How honorable that use sometimes was, my first quotation will testify.

I believe that all these three Persons [in the Godhead] are even in power and in *cunning* and in might, full of grace and of all goodness.

Foxe, *The Book of Martyrs; Confession of Faith, by William Thorpe.*

So the number of them, with their brethren, that were instructed in the songs of the Lord, even all that were *cunning*, was two hundred fourscore and eight.

1 *Chron.* xxv. 3. Authorized Version.

CURATE. Rector, vicar, every one having *cure* of souls, was a 'curate' once. Thus, 'bishops and *curates*' in the Liturgy.

They [the begging friars] letten *curats* to know Gods law by holding bookes fro them, and withdrawing of their vantages, by which they shulden have books and lerne.

Wiclif, *Treatise against the Friars*, p. 56.

Henry the Second of England commanded all prelates and *curates* to reside upon their dioceses and charges.

J. Taylor, *Ductor Dubitantium*, b. iii. c. 1.

Curate, a parson or vicar, one that serves a cure, or has the charge of souls in a parish.

Phillips, *The New World of Words.*

D.

DANGER, DANGEROUS. } A feudal term, beset with many difficulties in its passage to its present use. Du Cange has written upon it, and Diez, and there is a careful article in Richardson. It is a Low Latin word, 'dangerium,' of which the etymology is uncertain, signifying the strict right of the suzerain in regard to the fief of the vassal; thus, 'fief de *danger*,' a fief held under strict and severe conditions, and therefore in *danger* of being forfeited (juri stricto atque adeo confiscationi obnoxium; Du Cange). There is no difficulty here; but there is another early use of 'danger' and 'dangerous' which is not thus explained, nor yet the connection between it and the modern meaning of the words. I refer to that of 'danger' in the sense of 'coyness,' 'sparingness,' 'niggardliness,' and of 'dangerous' with the adjectival uses corresponding.

And if thy voice is faire and clere,
Thou shalt maken no great *daungere*,
When to singen they goodly pray;
It is thy worship for to obay.

Chaucer, *The Romaunt of the Rose*, 2317–2320.

We ourselves also were in times past unwise, disobedient, deceived, in *daunger* to lusts [δουλεύοντες ἐπιθυμίαις].

Tit. iii. 3. Tyndale.

Come not within his *danger* by thy will.

Shakespeare, *Venus and Adonis.*

My wages ben full streyt and eke ful smale;
My lord to me is hard and *daungerous.*

Chaucer, *The Friars Tale.*

But nathelesse, for his beaute
So fierce and *dangerous* was he,
That he nolde graunten her asking,
For weeping, ne for faire praying.

Id., *The Romaunt of the Rose*, 1480–1484.

Deadly. This and 'mortal' are often synonymes now; thus, 'a *deadly* wound' or 'a *mortal* wound:' but they are not invariably so; 'deadly' being always active, while 'mortal' is often passive, and signifying not that which inflicts death, but that which suffers death; thus, 'a *mortal* body,' or body subject to death, but not now 'a *deadly* body.' It was otherwise once. 'Deadly' is the constant word in Wiclif's Bible, wherever in the later versions 'mortal' occurs.

Elye was a *deedli* man lyk us, and in preier he preiede that it schulde not reyne on the erthe, and it reynede not three yeeris and sixe monethis.

Jam. v. 17. Wiclif.

Many holy prophets that were *deadly* men were martyred violently in the Old Law.

Foxe, *The Book of Martyrs; William Thorpe's Examination.*

DEFALCATION. A word at present of very slovenly and inaccurate use. We read in the newspapers of a 'defalcation' of the revenue, not meaning thereby an active lopping off ('defalcatio') of certain taxes with their proceeds, which would be the only correct use, but a passive falling short in its returns from what they previously were. Can it be that some confusion of 'defalcation' with 'default,' or at least a seeing of 'fault' and not 'falx' in its second syllable (there was once a verb 'to defalk'), has led to this?

My first crude meditations, being always hastily put together, could never please me so well at a second and more leisurable review, as to pass without some additions, *defalcations*, and other alterations, more or less.

Sanderson, *Sermons*, 1671, Preface.

As for their conjecture that Zorobabel, at the building of this temple purposely abated of those dimensions assigned by Cyrus, as too great for him to compass, in such *defalcation* of measures by Cyrus allowed; he showed little courtship to his master the emperor, and less religion to the Lord his God.

Fuller, *A Pisgah Sight of Palestine*, b. iii. c. 2.

DEFEND. Now to protect, but once to protect by prohibiting, or fencing round, to forbid, as 'défendre' is still in French.

The sin of maumetrie is the first that is *defended* in the Ten Commandments.

Chaucer, *The Parsons Tale.*

When can you say in any manner age
That ever God *defended* marriage?

Id., *The Wife of Baths Tale.*

DEFY, DEFIANCE. This means now to dare to the uttermost hostility, and so, as a consequence which will often follow upon this, to challenge. But in earlier use 'to defy' is, according to its etymology, to pronounce all bonds of *faith* and fellowship which existed previously between the defier and the defied to be wholly dissolved, so that nothing of treaty or even of the natural faith of man to man shall henceforth hinder extremest hostility between them. But still, when we read of one potentate sending 'defiance' to another, the challenge to conflict did not lie necessarily in the word, however such a message might provoke and would often be the prelude to this: it meant but the releasing of himself from all which hitherto had mutually obliged; and thus it came often to mean simply to disclaim, or renounce.

No man speaking in the Spirit of God *defieth* Jesus [λέγει ἀνάθεμα Ἰησοῦν].

1 *Cor.* xii. 3. Tyndale.

All studies here I solemnly *defy*,
Save how to gall and pinch this Bolingbroke.

Shakespeare, 1 *Henry IV.* Act i. Sc. 3.

There is a double people-pleasing. One sordid and servile, made of falsehood and flattery, which I *defy* and detest.

Fuller, *The Appeal of Injured Innocence*, p. 38.

Now although I instanced in a question which by good fortune never came to open *defiance*, yet there have been sects formed upon lighter grounds.

J. Taylor, *The Liberty of Prophesying*, § 3. 5.

DELAY. Like the French 'délayer,' used often in old time where we should now employ 'allay.' Out of an ignorance of this, and assuming it a misprint, some modern editors of our earlier authors have not scrupled to change 'delay' into 'allay.'

The watery showers *delay* the raging wind.

Surrey, *The Faithful Lover.*

Even so fathers ought to *delay* their eager reprehensions and cutting rebukes with kindness and clemency.

Holland, *Plutarch's Morals*, p. 16.

Cup-bearers know well enough and in that regard can discern and distinguish, when they are to use more or less water to the *delaying* of wines.

Id., *Ib.* p. 652.

DELICACY, DELICATELY, DELICIOUS, DELICIOUSLY. In the same way as self-indulgence creeps over us by unmarked degrees, so there creeps over the words that designate it a subtle change; they come to contain less and less of rebuke and blame; the thing itself being tolerated, nay allowed, it must needs be that the words which express it should be received into favor too. It has been thus, as I shall have occasion to note, with 'luxury;' it has been thus also with this whole group of words.

Thus much of *delicacy* in general; now more particularly of his first branch, gluttony.

Nash, *Christ's Tears over Jerusalem*, p. 140.

Cephisodorus, the disciple of Isocrates, charged him with *delicacy*, intemperance, and gluttony.

Blount, *Philostratus*, p. 229.

She that liveth *delicately* [σπαταλῶσα] is dead while she liveth.

1 *Tim.* v. 6. Authorized Version (margin).

Yea, soberest men it [idleness] makes *delicious*.

Sylvester, *Du Bartas*, *Second Week*, *Eden*.

How much she hath glorified herself and lived *deliciously* [ἐστρηνίασε], so much torment and sorrow give her.

Rev. xviii. 7. Authorized Version.

Demerit. It was plainly an inconvenient arrangement, a squandering of the wealth of the language, that 'merit' and 'demerit' should mean one and the same thing; however this might be justified by the fact that 'mereor' and 'demereor,' from which they were severally derived, were scarcely discriminated in meaning. It has thus come to pass, according to the desynonymizing processes ever at work in a language, that 'demerit' has ended in being employed only of *ill* desert, while 'merit' is left free to good or ill, having predominantly the sense of the former.

I fetch my life and being
From men of royal siege; and my *demerits*
May speak, unbonneted, to as proud a fortune
As this that I have reached.

Shakespeare, *Othello*, Act i. Sc. 2.

By our profane and unkind civil wars the world is grown to this pass, that it is reputed a singular *demerit* and gracious act, not to kill a citizen of Rome, but to let him live.

Holland, *Pliny*, vol i. p. 456.

But the Rhodians, contrariwise, in a proud humour of theirs, reckoned up a beadroll of their *demerits* toward the people of Rome.

Id., *Livy*, 1179.

DEMURE,
DEMURENESS. Used by our earlier writers without the insinuation, which is now always latent in it, that the external shows of modesty and sobriety rest upon no corresponding realities. On the contrary, the 'demure' was the truly modest and virtuous and the good. It is one of the many words to which the suspicious nature of man, with the warrants to a certain extent which these suspicions find, has given a turn for the worse.

These and other suchlike irreligious pranks did this Dionysius play, who notwithstanding fared no worse than the most *demure* and innocent, dying no other death than what usually other mortals do.

H. More, *The Antidote against Atheism*, b. iii. c. 1.

Which advantages God propounds to all the hearers of the Gospel, without any respect of works or former *demureness* of life, if so be they will but now come in and close with this high and rich dispensation.

Id., *On Godliness*, b. viii. c. 5.

In like manner women also in comely attire; with *demureness* [cum verecundiâ, Vulg.] and sobriety adorning themselves.

1 *Tim.* ii. 9. Rheims.

DEPART. Once used as equivalent with 'to separate'—a fact already forgotten, when, at the last revision of the Prayer-Book in 1661, the Puritan divines objected to the form as it then stood in the Marriage Service, 'till death us *depart;*' in condescension to whose objection the words, as we now have them, 'till death us *do part,*' were introduced.

And he schal *departe* hem atwynne, as a schepherde *departith* scheep fro kidus.

Matt. xxv. 32. Wiclif.

And whanne he hadde seid this thing, discencioun was made betwixe the farisies and the saduceis, and the multitude was *departid.*

Acts xxiii. 7. Id.

Neither did the apostles put away their wives, after they were called unto the ministry; but they continued with their wives lovingly and faithfully, till death *departed* them.

Becon, *An Humble Supplication unto God* (1554).

DEPRAVE. As 'pravus' is literally crooked, we may say that 'to deprave' was formerly 'untruly *to present* as crooked,' to defame; while it is now 'wickedly *to make* crooked.'

That lie, and cog, and flout, *deprave* and slander.

Shakespeare, *Much Ado about Nothing,* Act v. Sc. 1.

If affection lead a man to favour the less worthy in desert, let him do it without *depraving* or disabling the better deserver.

Bacon, *Essays,* 49.

I am *depraved* unjustly; who never deprived the Church of her authority.

Fuller, *The Appeal of Injured Innocence*, part i. p. 45.

DESIRE. 'To desire' is only to look *forward* with longing now; the word has lost the sense of regret or looking *back* upon the lost but still loved. This it once possessed in common with 'desiderium' and 'desiderare,' from which more remotely, and 'désirer,' from which more immediately, we derive it.

He [Jehoram] reigned in Jerusalem eight years, and departed without being *desired*.

2 *Chron*. xxi. 20. Authorized Version.

She that hath a wise husband must entice him to an eternal dearness by the veil of modesty and the grave robes of chastity, and she shall be pleasant while she lives, and *desired* when she dies.

J. Taylor, *The Marriage Ring*, Sermon 18.

DIGESTED. Scholars of the seventeenth century often employ a word of their own language in the same latitude which its equivalent possessed in the Greek or the Latin; as though it entered into all the rights of its equivalent, and corresponded with it on all points, because it corresponded in one. Thus, 'coctus' meaning 'digested,' why should not 'digested' mean all which 'coctus' meant? But one of the meanings of 'coctus' is 'ripened;' 'digested' therefore might be employed in the same sense.

Splendid fires, aromatic spices, rich wines, and well-*digested* fruits.

J. Taylor, *Discourse on Friendship*.

DISABLE. Our ancestors felt that to injure the character of another was the most effectual way of 'disabling' him; and out of a sense of this they often used 'disable' in the sense of to disparage, to speak slightingly of.

> Farewell, mounsieur traveller. Look, you lisp, and wear strange suits; *disable* all the benefits of your own country.
>
> Shakespeare, *As you like it*, Act iv. Sc. 1.

> If affection lead a man to favour the less worthy in desert, let him do it without depraving or *disabling* the better deserver.
>
> Bacon, *Essays*, 49.

DISCOURSE. It is very characteristic of the slight acquaintance with our elder literature—the most obvious source for elucidating Shakespeare's text—which was possessed by many of his commentators down to a late day, that the phrase 'discourse of reason,' which he puts into Hamlet's mouth, should have perplexed them so greatly. Gifford, a pitiless animadverter on the real or imaginary mistakes of others, and who tramples upon Warburton for attempting to explain this phrase as though Shakespeare had ever written it, declares, "'discourse *of* reason' is so poor and perplexed a phrase that I should dismiss it at once for what I believe to be his genuine language;" and then proceeds to suggest the obvious but erroneous correction "discourse *and* reason" (see his *Massinger*, vol. i. p. 148); while yet, if there be a phrase of frequent recurrence among the writers of our Elizabethan age and down to Milton, it is this. I have very little doubt that it occurs fifty times in Holland's translation of Plutarch's *Moralia*. What our fathers intended by 'discourse' and 'discourse of reason,' the following passages will abundantly declare.

There is not so great difference and distance between beast and beast, as there is odds in the matter of wisdom, *discourse* of reason, and use of memory between man and man.

Holland, *Plutarch's Morals*, p. 570; cf. pp. 313, 566, 570, 752, 955, 966, 977, 980.

You, being by nature given to melancholic *discoursing*, do easilier yield to such imaginations.

North, *Plutarch's Lives*, p. 830.

The other gods, and knights-at-arms, all slept, but only Jove
Sweet slumber seized not; he *discoursed* how best he might approve
His vow made for Achilles' grace.

Chapman, *Homer's Iliad*, b. ii.

As the intuitive knowledge is more perfect than that which insinuates itself into the soul gradually by *discourse*, so more beautiful the prospect of that building which is all visible at one view than what discovers itself to the sight by parcels and degrees.

Fuller, *The Worthies of England, Canterbury*.

Whence the soul
Reason receives, and reason is her being,
Discursive or intuitive; *discourse*
Is oftest yours, the latter most is ours.

Milton, *Paradise Lost*, b. v.

If you mean, by *discourse*, right reason, grounded on Divine Revelation and common notions, written by God in the hearts of all men, and deducing, according to the never-failing rules of logic, consequent deductions from them; if this be it which you mean by *discourse*, it is very meet and reasonable and necessary that men, as in all their actions, so especially in that of greatest importance, the choice of their way to happiness, should be left unto it.

Chillingworth, *The Religion of Protestants a Safe Way to Salvation*, Preface.

Disease. Our present limitation of 'disease' is a very natural one, seeing that nothing so effectually wars against ease as a sick and suffering condition of body. Still the limitation is modern, and by 'disease' was once meant any malease, distress, or discomfort whatever.

Wo to hem that ben with child, and nurishen in tho daies, for a greet *disese* [pressura magna, Vulg.] schal be on the erthe, and wrathe to this peple.

Luke xxi. 23. Wiclif.

Thy daughter is dead; why *diseasest* thou the master any further?

Mark v. 35. Tyndale.

This is now the fourteenth day they [the Cardinals] have been in the Conclave, with such pain and *disease* that your grace would marvel that such men as they would suffer it.

State Papers (*Letter to Wolsey from his Agent at Rome*), vol. vi. p. 182.

Dismal. Minshew's derivation of 'dismal,' that it is 'dies malus,' the unlucky, ill-omened day, is exactly one of those plausible etymologies to which one learns after a while to give no credit. Yet there can be no doubt that our fathers so understood the word, and that this assumed etymology often overrules their usage of it.

A buiterar or a maker of *dismal* days.

Deut. xviii. 10. Tyndale.

Then began they to reason and debate about the *dismal* days [tum de diebus religiosis agitari cœptum]. And the fifteenth day before the Kalends of August, so notorious for a twofold loss and overthrow, they set this unlucky mark upon it, that it should be reputed unmeet and unconvenient for any business, as well public as private.

Holland, *Livy*, p. 217

The particular calendars, wherein their [the Jews] good or *dismal* days are distinguished, according to the diversity of their ways, we find, Leviticus 26.

Jackson, *The Eternal Truth of Scriptures*, b. i. c. 22.

DIFFIDENCE, DIFFIDENTLY. } 'Diffidence' expresses now a not unbecoming distrust of one's own self, with only a slight intimation, such as 'verecundia' obtained in the silver age of Latin literature, that perhaps this distrust is carried too far; but it was once used for distrust of others, and sometimes for distrust pushed so far as to amount to an entire withholding of all faith from them, being nearly allied to despair; as, indeed, in *The Pilgrim's Progress*, Mistress 'Diffidence' is Giant Despair's wife.

Of the impediments which have been in the affections, the principle whereof hath been despair or *diffidence*, and the strong apprehension of the difficulty, obscurity, and infiniteness, which belongeth to the invention of knowledge.

Bacon, *Of the Interpretation of Nature*, c. 19.

Needless *diffidences*, banishment of friends.

Shakespeare, *King Lear*, Act i. Sc. 2.

Every sin smiles in the first address, and carries light in the face, and honey in the lip; but when we have well drunk, then comes that which is worse, a whip with ten strings, fears and terrors of conscience, and shame and displeasure, and a caitiff disposition, and *diffidence* in the day of death.

J. Taylor, *The Life of Christ*.

Mediators were not wanting that endeavoured a renewing of friendship between these two prelates, which the haughtiness, or perhaps the *diffidence* of Bishop Laud would not accept; a symptom of policy more than of grace, not to trust a reconciled enemy.

Hacket, *The Life of Archbishop Williams*, part ii. p. 86

It was by far the best course to stand *diffidently* against each other, with their thoughts in battle array.

Hobbes, *Thucydides*, b. iii. c. 83.

Disoblige. Release from obligation lies at the root of all uses, present and past, of this word; but it was formerly more the release from an oath or a duty, and now rather from the slighter debts of social life, to which kindness and courtesy on the part of another would have held us bound or obliged; while the contraries to these are 'disobliging.'

He did not think that Act of Uniformity could *disoblige* them [the Non-Conformists] from the exercise of their office.

Bates, *Mr. Richard Baxter's Funeral Sermon.*

He hath a very great obligation to do that and more; and he can noways be *disobliged*, but by the care of his natural relations.

J. Taylor, *Measures and Offices of Friendship.*

Document. Now used only of the *material*, and not, as once, of the *moral* proof, evidence, or means of instruction.

They were forthwith stoned to death, as a *document* unto others.

Sir W. Raleigh, *The History of the World*, b. v. c. 2. § 3.

Utterly to extirpate all trust in riches, where they abound, is only possible to the Omnipotent Power, and a rare *document* of divine mercy.

Jackson, *Justifying Faith*, b. iv. c. 6.

Dole. This and 'deal' are of course one and the same word, and answer to the German 'Theil,' a part or portion. It has now always the subaudition of a *scanty* portion, as 'to dole' is to deal scantily and reluctantly forth ('pittance' has acquired the same); but Sanderson's use of 'dole' is instructive, as showing that 'distribution or division' is all which once lay in the word.

There are certain common graces of illumination, and those indeed are given by *dole*, knowledge to one, to another tongues, to another healings; but it is nothing so with the special graces of sanctification. There is no distribution or division here; either all or none.

Sanderson, *Sermons*, 1671, vol. ii. p. 247.

DREADFUL. Now that which causes dread, but once that which felt it.

Forsothe the Lord shall gyve to thee there a *dreedful* herte and faylinge eyen.

Deut. xxviii. 65. Wiclif.

And to a grove faste ther beside
With *dredful* foot than stalketh Palamon.

Chaucer, *The Knightes Tale.*

DRENCH. As 'to *fell*' is 'to make to *fall*,' and 'to *lay*' 'to make to *lie*,' so 'to *drench*' is 'to make to *drink*,' though with a sense now very short of 'to drown;' but 'drench' and 'drown,' though desynonymized in our later English, were once perfectly adequate to one another.

They that wolen be maad riche, fallen in to temptacioun, and in to snare of the devil, and in to many unprofitable desiris and noyous, which *drenchen* men in to deth and perdicioun.

1 *Tim.* vi. 9. Wiclif.

> Well may men know it was no wight but he
> That kept the peple Ebraike fro *drenching*,
> With drye feet throughout the see passing.
>
> Chaucer, *The Man of Lawes Tale.*

Duke. One of Shakespeare's commentators charges him with an anachronism, the incongruous transfer of a modern title to an ancient condition of society, when he gives to Theseus the style of '*Duke* of Athens.' It would be of very little consequence if the charge were a true one; but it is not. 'Duke' has indeed since Shakespeare's time become that which this objector supposed it to have been always; but all were 'dukes' once who were 'duces,' captains and leaders of their people.

> He [St. Peter] techith christen men to be suget to kyngis and *dukis*, and to ech man for God.
>
> *Prologe on the first Pistel of Peter.* Wiclif.

> Hannibal, *duke* of Carthage.
>
> Sir T. Elyot, *The Governor*, b. i. c. 10.

> These were the *dukes* and princes of avail,
> That came from Greece.
>
> Chapman, *Homer's Iliad*, b. ii.

Dunce. I have sought elsewhere (*Study of Words*, p. 90) to trace somewhat at large the very curious history of this word. Sufficient here to say that Duns Scotus, whom Hooker styles "the wittiest of the school divines," has given us this name, which now ascribes hopeless ignorance, invincible stupidity, to him on whom it is affixed. The course by which this came to pass was as follows. When at the Reformation and Revival of Learning the works of the Schoolmen fell into extreme disfavor, at once with all the Reformers and with all votaries of the new learning, Duns, a standard-bearer among those, was so often referred to with scorn and contempt by these, that his name gradually became that byeword which now it is.

Remember ye not how within this thirty years, and far less, and yet dureth unto this day, the old barking curs, *Dunce's* disciples, and like draff called Scotists, the children of darkness, raged in every pulpit against Greek, Latin, and Hebrew?

Tyndale, *Works*, 1575, p. 278.

What *Dunce* or Sorbonist cannot maintain a parodox?

G. Harvey, *Pierce's Supererogation*, p. 159.

As for terms of honesty or civility, they are gibberish unto him, and he a Jewish Rabbin or a Latin *dunce* with him that useth any such form of monstrous terms.

Id., *Ib.*, p. 175.

Maud. Is this your tutor?
Tutor. Yes surely, lady;
I am the man that brought him in league with logic,
And read the *Dunces* to him.

Middleton, *A Chaste Maid in Cheapside*, Act iii. Sc. 1.

Dutch, Dutchman. Till late in the seventeenth century 'Dutch' ('deutsch' or 'teutsch,' 'theotiscus') meant generally 'German,' and a 'Dutchman' a native of Germany, while what we should now term a Dutchman would have been named then a Hollander. I observe it stated in a recent volume of travels in America, that in many parts there, Germans are now called 'Dutchmen,' the retention of an old usage, even as we find so many examples of this in America.

Though the root of the English language be *Dutch*, yet she may be said to have been inoculated afterwards upon a French stock.

Howell, *Lexicon Tetraglotton*, Preface.

Germany is slandered to have sent none to this war [the Crusades] at this first voyage; and that other pilgrims, passing through that country, were mocked by the *Dutch*, and called fools for their pains.

Fuller, *The Holy War*, b. i. c. 13.

At the same time began the *Teutonic* Order, consisting only of *Dutchmen*, well descended.

Id., *Ib.* b. ii. c. 16.

E.

EAGER, EAGERNESS. } The physical and literal sense of 'eager,' that is, sharp or acrid (aigre, acris), has quite departed from the word; which, however, occasionally retained this, long after it was employed in the secondary meaning which is its only one at present.

She was like thing for hunger dead,
That lad her life only by bread
Kneden with eisell* strong and *egre*.

Chaucer, *The Romaunt of the Rose*, 145–147.

Bees have this property by nature to find and suck the mildest and best honey out of the sharpest and most *eager* flowers.

Holland, *Plutarch's Morals*, p. 43.

Now on the *eager* razor's edge for life or death we stand.

Chapman, *Homer's Iliad*, 6–10.

* Vinegar.

Asproso, full of sourness or *eagerness*.

Florio, *New World of Words.*

Ebb. Nothing 'ebbs,' unless it be figuratively, except water now. But 'ebb,' oftener an adjective than any thing else, was continually used in our earlier English with a general meaning of shallow. There is still a Lancashire proverb, Cross the stream, where it is *ebbest.*

Orpiment, a mineral digged out of the ground in Syria, where it lieth very *ebb.*

Holland, *Pliny*, vol ii. p. 469.

This you may observe ordinarily in stones, that those parts and sides which lie covered deeper within the ground, be more frim and tender, as being preserved by heat, than those outward faces which lie *ebb*, or above the earth.

Id., *Plutarch's Morals*, p. 747.

It is all one whether I be drowned in the *ebber* shore, or in the midst of the deep sea.

Bishop Hall, *Meditations and Vows*, cent. ii.

Ecstasy. We still say of madmen that they are *beside themselves;* but 'ecstasy,' or a standing out of oneself, is no longer used as an equivalent to madness.

This is the very coinage of your brain,
This bodiless creation *ecstasy*
Is very cunning in.

Shakespeare, *Hamlet*, Act iii. Sc. 4.

Egregious. This has always now an ironical subaudition, which it was very far from having of old.

It may be denied that bishops were our first reformers, for Wickliffe was before them, and his *egregious* labours are not to be neglected.

Milton, *Animadversions upon the Remonstrants' Defence.*

Egregious viceroys of these eastern parts!

Marlowe, *Tamburlaine the Great,* Part ii. Act i. Sc. 1.

ELEVATE. There are two intentions with which any thing may be lifted from the place which now it occupies; either with the intention of setting it in a more conspicuous position; or else of removing it out of the way, or, figuratively, of withdrawing all importance and significance from it. We employ 'to elevate' now in the former intention; our ancestors for the most part, especially those whose style was influenced by their Latin studies, in the latter.

Withal, he forgat not to *elevate* as much as he could the fame of the foresaid unhappy field fought, saying, That if all had been true, there would have been messengers coming thick one after another upon their flight, to bring fresh tidings still thereof.

Holland, *Livy,* p. 1199.

Audience he had with great assent and applause; not more for *elevating* the fault and trespass of the common people, than for laying the weight upon those that were the authors culpable.

Id., *Ib.* p. 1207.

Tully in his oration Pro Flacco, to *elevate* or lessen that conceit which many Romans had of the nation of the Jews, objects little less unto them than our Saviour in this place doth, to wit that they were in bondage to the Romans.

Jackson, *Of the Primeval Estate of the First Man,* b. x. c. 14.

EMBEZZLE. We should say now that the Unjust Steward 'embezzled' his lord's goods (*Luke* xvi. 1);

but not that the Prodigal Son 'embezzled' the substance which he had received from his father (*Luke* xv. 13): yet the one would have been as free to our early writers as the other.

Go over towns and countries, tell the choice buildings, lands, and inheritances of them, and ask whose these were; all will tell you such a name, such a house enjoyed them, but now all is gone and *embezzled* away, not one acre remaining of four or five thousand pound lands by the year.

Rogers, *Matrimonial Honour*, p. 343.

Mr. Hackluit died, leaving a fair estate to an unthrift son, who *embezzled* it.

Fuller, *The Worthies of England, Herefordshire.*

The collection of these various readings [is] a testimony even of the faithfulness of these later ages of the Church, and of the high reverence they had to these records, in that they would not so much as *embesell* the various readings of them, but keep them still on foot for the prudent to judge of.

H. More, *On Godliness*, b. vii. c. 11.

Enormous, Enormity. } Now only applied to that which is irregular *in excess*, in this way transcending the established morm or rule. But departure from rule or regularities in *any* direction might be characterized as 'enormous' once.

Oh great corrector of *enormous* times,
Shaker of o'er-rank states, thou grand decider
Of dusty and old titles, that healst with blood
The earth when it is sick.

Beaumont and Fletcher, *The Two Noble Kinsmen*, Act v. Sc. 1.

Wild, without rule or art, *enormous* bliss.

Milton, *Paradise Lost.*

Pyramids, arches, obelisks, were but the *irregularities* of vain-glory, and wild *enormities* of ancient magnanimity.

Sir T. Browne, *Hydriotaphia.*

Ensure. None of our Dictionaries, as far as I can observe, have taken notice of an old use of this word, namely, to betroth, and thus to make *sure* the future husband and wife to each other.

After his mother Mary was *ensured* to Joseph, before they were coupled together, it was perceived she was with child.

Matt. i. 18. Sir John Cheke.

Albeit that she was by the king's mother and many other put in good comfort to affirm that she was *ensured* unto the king; yet when she was solemnly sworn to say the truth, she confessed that they were never *ensured.*

Sir T. More, *The History of King Richard III.*

Epicure. Now applied only to those who devote themselves, yet with a certain elegance and refinement, to the pleasures of the table. We may trace two earlier stages in its meaning. By Lord Bacon and others, the followers of Epicurus, whom we should call Epicuræans, are often called 'Epicures,' after the name of the founder of their sect. From them it was transferred to all who were, like them, deniers of a divine providence; and this is the common use of it by our elder divines. But inasmuch as those who have persuaded themselves that there is nothing above them, will seek their good, since men must seek it somewhere, in the things beneath them, in sensual delights, the name has been transferred, by that true moral instinct which is continually at work in speech, from the philosophical speculative atheist to the human swine, for whom the world is but a feeding-trough.

So the *Epicures* say of the Stoics' felicity placed in virtue, that it is like the felicity of a player, who if he were left of his auditors and their applause, he would straight be out of heart and countenance.

Bacon, *Colours of Good and Evil*, 3.

Aristotle is altogether an *Epicure;* he holdeth that God careth nothing for human creatures; he allegeth God ruleth the world like as a sleepy maid rocketh a child.

Luther, *Table-Talk*, c. 73.

The *Epicure* grants there is a God, but denies his providence.

Sydenham, *The Athenian Babbler*, 1627, p. 7.

EQUAL. The ethical sense of 'equal,' as fair, candid, just, has almost, if not altogether, departed from it.

O my most *equal* hearers, if these deeds
May pass with sufferance, what one citizen
But owes the forfeit of his life, yea, fame,
To him that dares traduce him.

Ben Jonson, *The Fox*, Act iv. Sc. 2.

Hear now, O house of Israel; is not my way *equal?* are not your ways unequal?

Ezek. xviii. 25. Authorized Version.

EQUIVOCAL, EQUIVOCALLY, EQUIVOCATION. The calling two or more different *things* by one and the same *name* (æque vocare) is the source of almost all error in human discourse. He who wishes to throw dust in the eyes of an opponent, to hinder his arriving at the real facts of a case, will often have recourse to this artifice, and thus 'to equivocate' and 'equivocation' have attained their present secondary meaning, very different from their original, which was simply the naming of two or more different things by one and the same word.

This visible world is but a picture of the invisible, wherein, as in a portrait, things are not truly, but in *equivocal* shapes, and as they counterfeit some real substance in that invisible fabric.

Sir T. Browne, *Religio Medici.*

Which [courage and constancy] he that wanteth is no other than *equivocally* a gentleman, as an image or a carcass is a man.

Barrow, *Sermon on Industry in our several Callings.*

He [the good herald] knows when indeed the names are the same, though altered through variety of writing in various ages, and where the *equivocation* is untruly affected.

Fuller, *The Holy State,* b. ii. c. 22.

All words, being arbitrary signs, are ambiguous; and few disputers have the jealousy and skill which is necessary to discuss *equivocations;* and so take verbal differences for material.

Baxter, *Catholic Theology,* Preface.

Essay. There is no particular modesty now in calling a treatise or dissertation an 'essay;' but from many passages it is plain that there was so once; which indeed is only agreeable to the proper meaning of the word, an 'essay' being a trial, proof, specimen, taste of a thing, rather than the very and completed thing itself.

To write just treatises requireth leisure in the writer, and leisure in the reader; and therefore are not so fit neither in regard of your highness' princely affairs, nor in regard of my continual service; which is the cause which hath made me choose to write certain brief notes, set down rather significantly than curiously, which I have called *Essays.* The word is late, but the thing is ancient.

Bacon, *Intended Dedication of his Essays to Prince Henry.*

Yet modestly he does his work survey,
And calls a finished poem an *essay.*

Dryden, *Epistle* 5, *To the Earl of Roscommon.*

EXEMPLARY. A certain vagueness in our use of 'exemplary' makes it for us little more than a loose synonym for excellent. We plainly often forget that 'exemplary' is strictly that which serves, or might serve, for an exemplar to others, while only through keeping this distinctly before us will passages like the following yield their exact meaning to us.

We are not of opinon therefore, as some are, that nature in working hath before her certain *exemplary* draughts or patterns.

Hooker, *Ecclesiastical Polity,* b. i. c. 3.

When the English, at the Spanish fleet's approach in eighty-eight [1588] drew their ships out of Plymouth haven, the Lord Admiral Howard himself towed a cable, the least joint of whose *exemplary* hand drew more than twenty men besides.

Fuller, *The Holy State,* b. iv. c. 17.

EXEMPLIFY. The use of 'exemplify' in the sense of the Greek παραδειγματίζειν (*Matt.* i. 19) has now passed away. Observe also in the passage quoted the curious use of 'traduce.'

He is a just and jealous God, not sparing to *exemplify* and traduce his best servants [*i. e.* when they sin], that their blur and penalty might scare all from venturing.

Rogers, *Matrimonial Honour*, p. 337.

EXPLODE. All our present uses of 'explode,' whether literal or figurative, have reference to bursting, and to bursting with noise; and it is for the most part forgotten, I should imagine, that these are all secondary and derived; that 'to explode,' originally an active verb, means to drive off the stage with loud clappings of the hands: and that when one of our early writers speaks of an 'exploded' heresy or an 'exploded opinion,' his image is not drawn from something which, having burst, has perished so; but he would imply that it has been contemptuously driven off from the world's stage — the fact that 'explosion' in this earlier sense was with a great noise being the connecting link between that sense and our present.

A third sort *explode* this opinion as trespassing on Divine Providence.

Fuller, *The Holy War*, b. iii. c. 18.

A man may with more facility avoid him that circumvents by money than him that deceives with glosing terms, which made Socrates so much abhor and *explode* them.

Burton, *The Anatomy of Melancholy; Democritus to the Reader.*

Shall that man pass for a proficient in Christ's school, who would have been *exploded* in the school of Zeno or Epictetus?

South, *Sermons*, vol. i. p. 431.

EXTERMINATE, EXTERMINATION. } It now signifies to destroy, to abolish; but our fathers, more true to the etymology, understood by it to drive men out of and beyond their own borders.

Most things do either associate and draw near to themselves the like, and do also drive away, chase, and *exterminate* their contraries.

Bacon, *Colors of Good and Evil*, 7.

We believe it to be the general interest of us all, as much as in us lies, with our common aid and succour to relieve our *exterminated* and indigent brethren.

Milton, *Letters written in Cromwell's name to the Evangelic cities of Switzerland, on occasion of the persecutions of the Vaudois.*

The state of the Jews was in that depression, in that conculcation, in that consternation, in that *extermination* in the captivity of Babylon.

Donne, *Sermons*, 19.

F.

FACETIOUS, FACETIOUSNESS. } It is certainly not a little remarkable that alike in Greek, Latin, and English, words expressive of witty festive conversation should have degenerated, though not all exactly in the same direction, and gradually acquired a worse signification than that with which they began; I mean εὐτραπελία, 'urbanitas,' and our own 'facetiousness;' this degeneracy of the words warning us how easily the thing itself degenerates; how sure it is to do so, to corrupt and spoil, if it be not seasoned with the only salt which will hinder this. 'Facetiousness' has already acquired the sense of buffoonery, of the making of ignoble mirth for others; there are plain indications that it will ere long acquire the sense of *indecent* buffoonery; while there was a time, as the examples given below will prove, when it could be ascribed in praise to high-bred ladies of the court and to grave prelates and divines.

He [Archbishop Williams] demonstrated that his mind was the lighter, because his friends were about him, and his *facetious* wit was true to him at those seasons, because his heart was true to his company.

Hacket, *The Life of Archbishop Williams*, part ii. p. 32.

A grave man, yet without moroseness, as who would willingly contribute his shot of *facetiousness* on any just occasion.

Fuller, *The Worthies of England, Oxfordshire.*

The king easily took notice of her [Anne Boleyn]; whether more captivated by the allurements of her beauty, or the *facetiousness* of her behaviour, it is hard to say.

Heylin, *The History of Queen Mary*, Introduction.

FAIRY. In whatever latitude we may employ 'fairy' now, it is always restricted to the middle beings of the *Gothic* mythology; being in no case applied, as it used to be, to the δαίμονες of classical antiquity.

Of the *fairy* Manto [daughter of Tiresias] I cannot affirm any thing of truth, whether she were a *fairy* or a prophetess.

Sir J. Harrington, *Orlando Furioso*, b. lxiii.

So long as these wise *fairies* Μοῖρα and Λάχεσις, that is to say Portion and Partition, had the ordering of suppers, dinners, and great feasts, a man should never see any illiberal or mechanical disorder.

Holland, *Plutarch's Morals*, p. 679.

FASTIDIOUS. Persons are 'fastidious' now, as feeling disgust; things, and indeed persons too, were 'fastidious' once, as occasioning disgust. The word has shifted from an objective to a subjective use. 'Fastidiosus' had both uses, but our modern quite predominated; indeed the other is very rare.

That thing for the which children be oftentimes beaten, is to them ever after *fastidious*.

Sir T. Elyot, *The Governor*, b. i. c. 9.

FEATURE. This, the Italian 'fattura,' is always the part now of a larger whole, a 'feature' of the landscape, the 'features' of the face; but there was no such limitation once; any thing made, any 'fattura,' was a 'feature' once.

We have not yet found them all [the scattered limbs of Truth], nor ever shall do, till her Master's second coming; He shall bring together every joint and member, and shall mould them into an immortal *feature* of loveliness and perfection.

Milton, *Areopagitica*.

So scented the grim *feature*, and upturned
His nostril wide into the murky air.

Id., *Paradise Lost*, x. 278.

But this young *feature* [a commentary on Scripture which Archbishop Williams had planned], like an imperfect embryo, was mortified in the womb by Star-chamber vexations.

Hacket, *The Life of Archbishop Williams*, part ii. p. 40.

FEMININE. The distinction between 'feminine' and 'effeminate,' that the first is 'womanly,' the second 'womanish,' the first what becomes a woman, and may under certain limitations without reproach be affirmed of a man, while the second is that which under all circumstances dishonors a man, as 'mannish' would dishonor a woman, is of comparatively modern growth.

> Till at the last God of veray right
> Displesed was with his condiciouns,
> By cause he [Sardanapalus] was in every mannes sight
> So *femynyne* in his affectiouns.
>
> Lydgate, *Poem against Idleness.*

> But Ninias being esteemed no man of war at all, but altogether *feminine*, and subjected to ease and delicacy, there is no probability in that opinion.
>
> Sir W. Raleigh, *The History of the World*, b. ii. c. 1. § 1.

> Commodus, the wanton and *feminine* son of wise Antoninus, gave a check to the great name of his father.
>
> J. Taylor, *Apples of Sodom.*

FIRMAMENT. We now use 'firmament' only for that portion of the sky on all sides visible above the horizon, having gotten this application of the word from the Vulgate (*Gen* i. 6), or at any rate from the Church Latin ('*firmamentum* cæleste,' Tertullian, *De Bapt.* iii.), as that had derived it from the Septuagint. This by στερέωμα had sought to express the firmness and stability of the sky-tent, which phenomenally (and scripture for the most part speaks phenomenally), is drawn over the earth; and to reproduce the force of the original Hebrew word — in which, however, there is rather the notion of expansion than of firmness (see H. More, *Defence of Cabbula*, p. 60). But beside this use of 'firmament,' totally strange to the classical 'firmamentum,' being derived to us from the ecclesiastical employment of the word, there is also an occasional use of it by the scholarly writers of the seventeenth century in the original classical sense, as generally that which makes strong or confirms.

I thought it good to make a strong head or bank to rule and guide the course of the waters; by setting down this position or *firmament*, namely, that all knowledge is to be limited by religion, and to be referred to use and action.

Bacon, *Of the Interpretation of Nature.*

Custom is the sanction, or the *firmament* of the law.

J. Taylor, *Apples of Sodom.*

Flicker. This and 'flutter' are thoroughly desynonymized now; a flame 'flickers,' a bird 'flutters;' but it was not so once.

But being made a swan,
With snowy feathers in the air to *flicker* he began.

Golding, *Ovid's Metamorphosis*, b. vii.

Flirt. Much more serious charges were implied once in this name than are at the present, as will be sufficiently clear from the quotations which follow.

For why may not the mother be naught, a peevish drunken *flurt*, a waspish choleric slut, a crazed piece, a fool, as soon as the nurse?

Burton, *The Anatomy of Melancholy*, part i. sect. 2.

Gadrouillette, *f.* A minx, giggle, *flirt*, callet, gixie; (a feigned word, applicable to any such cattell).

Cotgrave, *A French and English Dictionary*, 1660.

Fondling. 'Fond' retains to this day, at least in

poetry, not seldom the sense of foolish; but a 'fondling' is no longer a fool.

An epicure hath some reason to allege, an extortioner is a man of wisdom, and acteth prudently in comparison to him; but this *fondling* [the profane swearer] offendeth heaven and abandoneth happiness he knoweth not why or for what.

Barrow, *Sermon* 15.

We have many such *fondlings*, that are their wives' pack-horses and slaves.

Burton, *The Anatomy of Melancholy*, part iii. sect. 3.

Forlorn Hope. There are two points of difference between the past use of 'forlorn hope' and the present. The first, that it was seldom used—I can not myself recall a single example—in that which is now its only application, namely, of those who, being the first to mount the breach, thus set their lives upon a desperate hazard; but always of the skirmishers and others thrown out in front of an army about to engage. Here indeed the central notion of the word may be said to be the same as it is now. These first come to hand-strokes with the enemy; they bear the brunt of their onset; and there may therefore seem less likelihood that they will escape than those who come after. This is quite true, and it comes remarkably out in one of my quotations from Holland. But in passages innumerable this of the greater hazard to which the 'forlorn hope' are exposed, has noticeably enough quite disappeared from the phrase, and they are simply that part of the army which, being posted in the front, commences the engagement. In this sense it is often merely the 'forlorn,' 'hope' being omitted.* It would be curious to know when 'forlorn hope' first appeared in the language. The first example I find of it is in Gascoigne's *Fruits of War*, st. 74.

These [the Roman Velites] were loose troops, answerable in a manner to those which we call now by a French name Enfans Perdues, but when we use our own terms, *The Forlorn Hope.*

Sir W. Raleigh, *The History of the World,* b. v. c. 3, § 8.

Before the main battle of the Carthaginians he sets the auxiliaries and aid-soldiers, a confused rabble and medley of all sorts of nations, who, as the *forlorn hope,* bearing the furious heat of the first brunt, might, if they did no other good, yet with receiving many a wound in their bodies dull and turn the edge of the enemy's sword.

Holland, *Livy,* p. 765.

Upon them the light-armed *forlorn hope* [qui primi agminis erant] of archers and darters of the Roman host, which went before the battle to skirmish, charged forcibly with their shot.

Id., *Ib.* p. 641; cf. 1149, 1150, 1195.

Christ's descent into hell was not ad prædicandum, to preach; useless, where his auditory was all the *forlorn hope.*

Fuller, *The Worthies of England, Hampshire.*

FORMALITY. It was observed above on the phrase, 'common sense,' that a vast number of our words have descended to us from abstruse sciences and speculations, we accepting them often in a total uncon-

* The fearful are in the *forlorn* of those that march for hell.

Gurnall, *The Christian in Complete Armour,* c. 1.

They [the Enniskillen horse] offered with spirit to make always the *forlorn* of the army.

Dryden's Works (Scott's edition), vol. vii. p. 303.

sciousness of the quarter from which they come. Another proof of this assertion is here; only as it was metaphysics there, it is logic here which has given us the word. It is curious to trace the steps by which 'formality,' which meant in the language of the schools the essentiality, the innermost heart of a thing, should now mean something not merely so different, but so opposite.

According to the rule of the casuists, the *formality* of prodigality is inordinateness of our laying out, or misbestowing on what we should not.

Whitlock, *Zootomia*, p. 497.

When the school makes pertinacy or obstinacy to be the *formality* of heresy, they say not true at all, unless it be meant the obstinacy of the will and choice; and if they do, they speak impertinently and inartificially, this being but one of the causes that makes error become heresy; the adequate and perfect *formality* of heresy is whatsoever makes the error voluntary and vicious.

J. Taylor, *The Liberty of Prophesying*, § 2. 10.

France, Frenchman. We consider now, and consider rightly, that there was properly no 'France' before they were Franks; and, speaking of the land or people before the Frankish immigration, we use Gaul, Gauls, and Gaulish; just as we speak of Cæsar's invasion of Britain, not his invasion of England: our fathers had no such scruples.

When Cæsar saw his army prone to war,
And fates so bent, lest sloth and long delay
Might cross him, he withdrew his troops from *France*,
And in all quarters musters men for Rome.

Marlowe, *The First Book of Lucan*.

A *Frenchman* together with a *Frenchwoman*, likewise a Grecian man and woman, were let down alive in the beast-market into a vault under the ground, stoned all about.

Holland, *Livy*, p. 467.

Frightful. Now always active, that which inspires fright; but formerly as often passive, that which is, or is liable to be, frightened.

The wild and *frightful* herds,
Not hearing other noise but this of chattering birds,
Feed fairly on the lawns.

Drayton, *Polyolbion.*

Frippery. Now such trumpery, such odds and ends of cheap finery, as one might expect to meet at an old-clothes shop; but in our early dramatists and others of their time, the shop itself where old clothes were scoured, 'interpolated,' and presented anew for sale (officina vestium tritarum, Skinner); nor had 'frippery' then the contemptuous subaudition of worthlessness in the objects offered for sale which its present use would imply.

Enter Luke, with shoes, garters, fans, and roses.
Gold. Here he comes, sweating all over,
He shows like a walking *frippery*.

Massinger, *The City Madam*, Act i. Sc. 1.

Hast thou foresworn all thy friends in the Old Jewry? or dost thou think us all Jews that inhabit there? Yet, if thou dost, come over, and but see our *frippery*. Change an old shirt for a whole smock with us.

Ben Jonson, *Every Man in his Humour*, Act i. Sc. 1.

FULSOME, FULSOMENESS. I have seen it questioned whether in the first syllable of 'fulsome' we are to find 'foul' or 'full.' There should be no question on the matter: seeing that 'fulsome' is properly no more than 'full,' and then secondly that which by its fulness and overfulness produces first satiety, and then loathing and disgust. This meaning of 'fulsome' is still retained in our only present application of the word, namely, to compliments and flattery, which by their grossness produce this effect on him who is their object; but the word had once many more applications than this.

His lean, pale, hoar, and withered corpse grew *fulsome*, fair, and fresh.

Golding, *Ovid's Metamorphosis*, b. vii.

The next is Doctrine, in whose lips there dwells
A spring of honey, sweeter than its name,
Honey which never *fulsome* is, yet *fills*
The widest souls.

Beaumont, *Psyche*, b. xix. st. 210.

Making her soul to loathe dainty meat, or putting a surfeit and *fulsomeness* into all which she enjoys.

Rogers, *Naaman the Syrian*, p. 32.

Chaste and modest as he [Persius] is esteemed, it cannot be denied but that in some places he is broad and *fulsome*. No decency is considered; no *fulsomeness* omitted.

Dryden, *Dedication of Translations from Juvenal.*

G.

GARB. This is one of many words, whereof all the meaning has run to the surface. A man's dress was once only a portion, and a very small portion of his 'garb,' which included his whole outward presentment to other men; now it is all.

> First, for your *garb*, it must be grave and serious,
> Very reserved and locked; not tell a secret
> On any terms, not to your father.
>
> Ben Jonson, *The Fox*, Act iv. Sc. 1.

> The greatest spirits, and those of the best and noblest breeding, are ever the most respective and obsequious in their *garb*, and the most observant and grateful in their language to all.
>
> Feltham, *Resolves*, lxxv.

> A σεμνοπρέπεια in his person, a grave and a smiling *garb* compounded together to bring strangers into a liking of their welcome.
>
> Hacket, *The Life of Archbishop Williams*, part ii. p. 32.

GARBLE. Books only are 'garbled' now; and 'garbled' extracts are extracts which have been dishonestly made, which have been so shifted, mutilated, and otherwise dealt with, that, while they are presented as fair specimens, they convey a false impression. It is not difficult to trace the downward progress of the word. It is derived from the low Latin 'garba,' a wheatsheaf, and 'garbellare,' to sift or cleanse corn from any dust or rubbish which may have become mingled with it. It was then applied to any separation of the good from the bad, retaining that, rejecting this, and used thus especially of spices; then generally to picking and choosing, but without any intention to select the better and to dismiss the worse; and lastly, as at present, to picking and choosing with the distinct purpose of selecting the worse, and dismissing the better. It is a very favorite word in its earlier uses with Fuller.

Garbling of bow-staves (anno 1 R. 3, cap. 11) is the sorting or culling out of the good from the bad.

Cowell, *The Interpreter*, s. v.

There was a fair hospital, built to the honour of St. Anthony in Bennet's Fink, in this city; the protectors and proctors whereof claimed a privilege to themselves, to *garble* the live pigs in the markets of the city; and such as they found starved or otherwise unwholesome for man's sustenance they would slit in the ear, tie a bell about their necks, and turn them loose about the city.

Fuller, *The Worthies of England, London.*

Garbling men's manners you did well divide,
To take the Spaniards' wisdom, not their pride.
With French activity you stored your mind,
Leaving to them their fickleness behind;
And soon did learn, your temperance was such,
A sober industry even from the Dutch.

Id., *The Worthies of England; A Panegyric on Charles II.*

To *garble*, to cleanse from dross and dirt, as grocers do their spices, to pick or cull out.

Phillips, *The New World of Words.*

GARLAND. At present we know no other 'garlands' but of flowers; but 'garland' was at one time a technical name for the royal crown or diadem, and not a poetical one, as might at first sight appear; as witness these words of Matthew of Paris in his *Life of Henry III.*: Rex veste deauratâ, et coronulâ aureâ, quæ vulgariter *garlanda* dicitur, redimitus.

In the adoption and obtaining of the *garland*, I being seduced and provoked by sinister counsel did commit a naughty and abominable act.

Grafton, *Chronicle of King Richard III.*

In whose [Edward the Fourth's] time, and by whose occasion, what about the getting of the *garland*, keeping it, losing and winning again, it hath cost more English blood than hath twice the winning of France.

Sir T. More, *The History of King Richard III.*, p. 107.

What in me was purchased,
Falls unto thee in a more fairer sort;
So thou the *garland* wear'st successively.

Shakespeare, 2 *Henry IV.* Act iv. Sc. 4.

GAZETTE. An Italian word, signifying originally, as is well known, a small piece of tin money current at Venice; which being the price at which the flying sheets of news, first published there, were sold, in this way gave to them their name; and they also were called 'gazettes.' We see the word in this its secondary sense, but not as yet thoroughly at home in English, for it still retains an Italian termination, in Ben Jonson's *Volpone* (Act v. Sc. 2), of which the scene is laid at Venice. Curiously enough the same play gives also an example, quoted below, of the word in its earlier use.

If you will have a stool, it will cost you a *gazet*, which is almost a penny.

Coryat, *Crudities*, vol. ii. p. 15.

What monstrous and most painful circumstance
Is here to get some three or four *gazettes*,
Some threepence in the whole.

Ben Jonson, *Volpone*, Act ii. Sc. 1.

GELDING. Restrained at present to horses which have ceased to be entire; but until 'eunuch,' which is of somewhat late adoption, had been introduced into the language, serving the turns which that serves now.

Thanne Joseph was lad into Egepte, and bought him Potiphar, the *gelding* of Pharao.

Gen. xxxix. 1. Wiclif.

And whanne thei weren come up of the water, the spirit of the Lord ravyschid Filip, and the *geldynge* say hym no more.

Acts viii. 39. Wiclif.

Lysimachus was very angry, and thought great scorn that Demetrius should reckon him a *gelding*.

North, *Plutarch's Lives*, p. 741.

GENEROSITY. We still use 'generous' occasionally in the sense of highly or nobly born; but 'generosity' has quite lost this its earlier sense, and acquired a purely ethical meaning.

Nobility began in thine ancestors, and ended in thee; and the *generosity* that they gained by virtue, thou hast blotted by vice.

Lyly, *Euphues and his England.*

Their eyes are commonly black and small, noses little, nails almost as long as their fingers, but serving to distinguish their *generosity*.

Harris, *Voyages*, vol. i. p. 465.

GESTATION. Now a technical word applied only to the period during which the females of animals carry their young; but acknowledging no such limitation once.

Gestation in a chariot or wagon hath in it a shaking of the body, but some vehement, and some more soft.

Sir T. Elyot, *The Castle of Health*, b. ii. c. 34.

Gestation, an exercise of the body, by being carried in coach, litter, upon horseback, or in a vessel on the water.

Holland, *Pliny*, *The Explanation of the Words of Art.*

GLORY. }
GLORIOUS. } 'Glory' is never employed now in the sense of '*vain*-glory,' nor 'glorious' in that of '*vain*-glorious,' as once they often were.

In military commanders and soldiers *vain-glory* is an essential point; for as iron sharpens iron, so by *glory* one courage sharpeneth another.

Bacon, *Essays*, 54.

So commonly actions begun in *glory* shut up in shame.

Bishop Hall, *Contemplations*, *On Babel.*

Some took this for a *glorious* brag; others thought he [Alcibiades] was like enough to have done it.

North, *Plutarch's Lives*, p. 183.

Likewise *glorious* followers, who make themselves as trumpets of the commendation of those they follow, are full of inconvenience; for they taint business through want of secrecy, and they export honour from a man and make him a return in envy.

Bacon, *Essays*, 48.

He [Anselm] little dreamt then that the weeding-hook of Reformation would after two ages pluck up his *glorious* poppy [prelacy] from insulting over the good corn [presbytery].

Milton, *The Reason of Church Government*, b. i. c. 5.

Good nature. As Metaphysics have yielded us 'common sense,' and logic 'formality,' so we owe to theology 'good nature.' By it our elder divines understood far more than we understand by it now; even all which it is possible for a man to have without having the grace of God. The contrast between grace and nature was of course unknown to the Greeks; but, this being kept in mind, we may say that the 'good nature' of our old theology was as as nearly as possible expressed by the εὐφυΐα of Aristotle (*Eth. Nic.* iii. 7), the genial preparedness for the reception of every high teaching.

Good nature, being the relics and remains of that shipwreck which Adam made, is the proper and immediate disposition to holiness. When *good nature* is heightened by the grace of God, that which was natural becomes now spiritual.

J. Taylor, *Sermon preached at the Funeral of Sir George Dalstone.*

Good nature! alas, where is it? Since Adam fell, there was never any such thing in rerum naturâ; if there be any good thing in any man, it is all from grace. That thing which we use to call *good nature* is indeed but a subordinate means or instrument, whereby God restraineth some men more than others from their birth, and special constitution, from sundry outrageous exorbitances, and so is a branch of this restraining grace whereof we now speak.

Sanderson, *Sermons*, 1671, vol. i. p. 279.

If any good did appear in the conversation of some men who followed that religion [the Pagan], it is not to be imputed to the influence of that, but to some better cause; to the relics of *good nature*, to the glimmerings of natural light, or (perhaps also) to secret whispers and impressions of divine grace on some men's minds, vouchsafed in pity to them.

Barrow, *Sermon* 14 *on the Apostles' Creed.*

They [infidels] explode all natural differences of good and evil;

deriding benignity, mercy, pity, gratitude, ingenuity; that is, all instances of *good nature*, as childish and silly dispositions.

Id., *Sermon* 6 *on the Apostles' Creed.*

GOSPELLER. Now seldom used save in ritual language, and there designating the priest or deacon who in the divine service reads the Gospel of the day; but once used as equivalent to Evangelist, and subsequently applied to adherents of the Reformed faith; both which meanings have since departed from it.

Mark, the *gospeller*, was the goostli sone of Petre in baptysm.

Wiclif, *The Prologe of Marke.*

The persecution was carried on against the *gospellers* with much fierceness by those of the Roman persuasion.

Strype, *Memorials of Archbishop Cranmer*, b. iii. c. 16.

GOSSIP. It would be interesting to collect instances in which the humbler classes of society have retained the correct use of a word, which has been let go by those who would rather claim to be guardians of the purity of their native tongue. 'Gossip' is one, being still used by our peasantry in its first and etymological sense, namely, as a sponsor in baptism—one *sib* or akin in *God*, according to the doctrine of the medieval Church, that sponsors contracted a spiritual affinity with one another, with the parents, and with the child itself. 'Gossips,' in this primary sense, would ordinarily be intimate and familiar with one another—would have been so already, or through this affinity would have become so; and thus the word was next applied to all familiars and intimates. At a later day it obtained the meaning which is now predominant in it, namely, the idle, profitless talk, the 'commérage' (which word has exactly the same history), that too often finds place in the intercourse of such.

They had mothers as we had; and those mothers had *gossips* (if their children were christened) as we are.

Ben Jonson, *The Staple of News, The Induction.*

Thus fareth the golden mean, through the misconstruction of the extremes. Well-tempered zeal is lukewarmness; devotion is hypocrisy; charity, ostentation; constancy, obstinacy; gravity, pride; humility, abjection of spirit; and so go through the whole parish of virtues, where misprision and envy are *gossips*, be sure the child shall be nicknamed.

Whitlock, *Zootomia*, p. 3.

Should a great lady that was invited to be a *gossip*, in her place send her kitchen-maid, 'twould be ill taken.

Selden, *Table-Talk, Prayer.*

Gravel. This verb has lost now any but a secondary and figurative meaning. But the way in which 'to be gravelled' should mean to be utterly perplexed and brought to an intellectual standstill, the passage quoted below will show.

And when we were fallen into a place between two seas, they *gravelled* the ship [*impegerunt* navem, Vulg.].

Acts xxvii. 41. Rheims.

Grudge. Now to repine at the good which others already have, or which we may be required to impart to them; but it formerly implied *open* utterances of discontent and displeasure with others, and did the work which 'to murmur' does now. Traces of this still survive in our English Bible.

And the farisies and scribis *gruechiden;* seiynge for this resceyveth synful men and eteth with hem.

Luke xv. 2. Wiclif.

Yea without *grudging* Christ suffered the cruel Jews to crown Him with most sharp thorns, and to strike Him with a reed.

Foxe, *The Book of Martyrs; Examination of William Thorpe.*

Use hospitality one to another without *grudging* [ἄνευ γογγυσμῶν].

1 *Pet.* iv. 9. Authorized Version.

GROPE. Now to feel *for*, and uncertainly, as does a blind man or one in the dark; but once simply to feel, to gripe or grasp.

Handis thei hav, and thei shal not *grope* [et non *palpabunt,* Vulg.].

Ps. cxiii. 7. Wiclif.

I have touched and tasted the Lord, and *groped* Him with hands, and yet unbelief have made all unsavoury.

Rogers, *Naaman the Syrian,* p. 231.

GUARD. Is 'guard,' in the sense of welt or border to a garment, nothing more than a *special* application of 'guard,' as it is familiar to us all? or is it altogether a different word with its own etymology, and only by accident offering the same letters in the same sequence? I have assumed, though not with perfect confidence, the former; for indeed otherwise the word would have no right to a place here.

Antipater wears in outward show his apparel with a plain white welt or *guard*, but he is within all purple, I warrant you, and as red as scarlet.

Holland, *Plutarch's Morals*, p. 412.

Then were the fathers of those children glad men to see their sons apparelled like Romans, in fair long gowns, *garded* with purple.

North, *Plutarch's Lives*, p. 492.

Give him a livery
More *guarded* than his fellows.

Shakespeare, *The Merchant of Venice*, Act ii. Sc. 2.

H.

Hag. One of the many words which, applied formerly to both sexes, are now restrained only to one. Our Dictionaries take no notice of the wider use of the word.

And that old *hag* [Silenus] that with a staff his staggering limbs doth stay,
Scarce able on his ass to sit for reeling every way.

Golding, *Ovid's Metamorphosis*, b. iv.

Handsome, Handsomeness. Now referred exclusively to comeliness, either literal or figurative. It is of course closely connected with 'handy,' indeed differs from it only in termination, and in all early uses means having prompt and dexterous use of the hands, and then generally able, adroit. In Cotgrave's *French and English Dictionary*, 'habile,' 'adroit,' 'maniable,' take precedence of 'beau,' 'belle,' as French equivalents of it.

Few of them [the Germans] use swords or great lances; but carry javelins with a narrow and short iron, but so sharp and *handsome*, that, as occasion serveth, with the same weapon they can fight both at hand and afar off.

Greenwey, *Tacitus*, vol. i. 259.

A light footman's shield he takes unto him, and a Spanish blade by his side, more *handsome* to fight short and close [ad propiorem *habili* pugnam].

Holland, *Livy*, p. 255.

Philopœmen sought to put down all exercise, which made men's bodies unmeet to take pains, and to become soldiers to fight in defence of their country, that otherwise would have been very able and *handsome* for the same.

North, *Plutarch's Lives*, p. 306.

Both twain of them made haste,
And girding close for *handsomeness* their garments to their waist,
Bestirred their cunning hands apace.

Golding, *Ovid's Metamorphosis*, b. vi.

Harbinger. This word belongs at present to our poetical λέξις, and to that only; its original significance being nearly or quite forgotten, as is evident from the inaccurate ways in which it has come to be used; as though a 'harbinger' were merely one who announced the coming, and not always one who prepared a place and lodging, a 'harbor,' for another. He did indeed announce the near approach, but only as an accidental consequence of his office. Our Lord, if we may reverently say it, precisely assumed to Himself the office of a 'harbinger,' when He said, "I go to prepare a place for you" (*John* xiv. 2).

There was a *harbinger* who had lodged a gentleman in a very ill room; who expostulated with him somewhat rudely; but the *harbinger* carelessly said, "You will take pleasure in it when you are out of it."

Bacon, *Apothegms.*

I'll be myself the *harbinger*, and make joyful
The hearing of my wife with your approach.

Shakespeare, *Macbeth,* Act i. Sc. 4.

The fame of Frederick's valour and maiden fortune, never as yet spotted with ill success, like a *harbinger* hastening before, had provided victory to entertain him at his arrival.

Fuller, *The Holy War,* b. iii. c. 31.

HARDY, HARDILY. When used of *persons*, 'hardy' means always now enduring, indifferent to fatigue, hunger, thirst, heat, cold, and the like. But it had once a far more prevailing sense of bold, which now only remains to it in connection with *things*, as we should still speak of a 'hardy,' meaning thereby a bold, assertion; though never now of a 'hardy,' if we intended a bold or daring person. In respect of the quotation from Lord Bacon, the reader must bear in mind that his Charles the *Hardy* is Charles le *Téméraire*, or Charles the *Bold*, as we always style him now.

Hap helpeth *hardy* man alway, quoth he.

Chaucer, *The Legend of Good Women.*

It is not to be forgotten what Commineus observeth of his first master, duke Charles the *Hardy*, namely, that he would communicate his secrets with none.

Bacon, *Essays,* 27.

Hardily [audacter, Vulg.] he entride in to Pilat, and axide the body of Jhesu.

Mark xv. 43. Wiclif.

Harlot. I have no desire to entangle myself in the question of this word's etymology; it is sufficient to observe that it was used of both sexes alike; and though for the most part a word of slight and contempt, implied nothing of that special *form* of sin to which it exclusively refers at the present.

> A sturdy *harlot* went hem ay behind,
> That was his hostes man, and bare a sakke,
> And what men gave him, laid it on his bakke.

Chaucer, *The Sompnoures Tale.*

No man but he and thou and such other false *harlots* praiseth any such preaching.

Foxe, *The Book of Martyrs; The Examination of William Thorpe.*

About this time [A. D. 1264] a redress of certain sects was intended, among which one by name specially occurreth, and called the assembly of *harlots*,* a kind of people of a lewd disposition and uncivil.

Id., *Ib.* vol. i. p. 435.

Harness. In French the difference between the 'harness' of a man and of a horse is expressed by a slight difference in the spelling, 'harnois' in one case, 'harnais' in the other. In English we only retain it now in the second of these applications.

* 'Qui se *harlotos* appellant' are the important words in Henry the Third's letter to the Sheriff of Oxfordshire, requiring their dispersion.

But when a stronger than he cometh upon him and overcometh him, he taketh from him his *harness* wherein he trusted, and divideth his goods.

Luke xi. 22. Tyndale.

Those that sleep in Jesus shall God bring with Him, and *harness* them with the bright armour of life and immortality.

H. More, *The Grand Mystery of Godliness*, b. iv. c. 18.

HARVEST. It is remarkable that while spring, summer, winter, have all their Anglo Saxon names, we designate the other quarter of the year by its Latin title 'autumn;' the word which should have designated it, 'harvest,' 'hearfest' (= the German 'Herbst'), having been appropriated to the ingathering of the *fruits* of this season, not to the season itself. In this indeed we are truer to the proper meaning of 'harvest' than the Germans, who have transferred the word from the former to the latter; for it is closely related with the Greek καρπός and the Latin 'carpo.' Occasionally, however, as in the passage which follows, 'harvest' assumes with us also the signification of autumn.

There stood the Springtime with a crown of fresh and fragrant flowers;
There waited Summer naked stark, all save a wheaten hat;
And *Harvest* smeared with treading grapes late at the pressing fat;
And lastly quaking for the cold stood Winter all forlorn.

Golding, *Ovid's Metamorphosis*, b. ii.

HEAR. Our scholars of the seventeenth century occasionally use the Latin idiom, 'to hear well,' or 'to hear ill,' *i. e.* concerning oneself (bene audire, male audire), instead of to be praised, or to be blamed.

[Fabius] was well aware, that not only within his own camp, but also now at Rome, he *heard ill* for his temporizing and slow proceedings.

Holland, *Livy*, p. 441.

What more national corruption, for which England *hears ill* abroad, than household gluttony?

Milton, *Areopagitica*, p. 431.

The abbot made his mind known to the Lord Keeper, that he would gladly be present in the Abbey of Westminster on our Christmas-day in the morning, to behold and hear how that great feast was solemnized in our congregations, which *heard* very *ill* beyond the seas for profaneness.

Hacket, *The Life of Archbishop Williams*, part i. p. 210

HOBBY. The 'hobby' being the ambling nag ridden for pleasure, and then the child's toy in imitation of the same, had in these senses nearly passed out of use, when the word revived, by a very natural transfer, in the sense which it now has, of a favorite pursuit which carries a man easily and pleasantly forward.

The French lackey and Irish footboy shrugging at the door, with their master's *hobby*-horses, to ride to the new play.

Decker, *The Gull's Hornbook*, c. 5.

King Agesilaus, having a great sort of little children, was one day disposed to solace himself among them in a gallery where they played, and took a little *hobby*-horse of wood, and bestrid it.

Puttenham, *The Art of English Poesy*, b. iii. c. 24.

A *hobby*-horse, or some such pretty toy,
A rattle would befit you better, boy.

Randolph, *Poems*, p. 19.

HOMELY. The etymology of 'homely' which Milton puts into the mouth of Comus—

> "It is for *homely* features to keep *home;*
> They had their name hence"—

witnesses that in his time it had the same meaning which it now has. At an earlier day, however, it much more nearly corresponded to the German 'heimlich,' that is, secret, inward, familiar, as those may be presumed to be that share in a common *home.*

And the enemyes of a man ben thei that ben *homeli* with him.
Matt. x. 36. Wiclif; cf. *Judges* xix. 4, and often.

> God grant thee thine *homly* fo to espie;
> For in this world n'is werse pestilence
> Than *homly* fo, all day in thy presence.
> Chaucer, *The Merchantes Tale.*

With all these men I was right *homely,* and communed with them long time and oft.
Foxe, *The Book of Martyrs; The Examination of William Thorpe.*

HOYDEN. Now and for a long time since a clownish, ill-bred *girl;* yet I cannot doubt that Skinner is right when he finds in it only another form of 'heathen.' Remote as the words appear at starting, it will not be hard to bring them close together. In the first place, it is only by a superinduced meaning that 'heathen' has its present sense of non-Christian; it is properly, as Grimm has abundantly shown, a dweller on the heath; then any living a wild, savage life: thus, we have in Wiclif *(Acts* xxviii. 1), "And *hethen* men [barbari, Vulg.] dide unto us not litil curtesie;" and only afterward was the word applied to those who resisted to the last the humanizing influences of the Christian faith. This 'heathen' is in Dutch 'heyden;' while less than two hundred years ago 'hoyden' was by no means confined, as it now is, to the female sex, the clownish, ill-bred *wench*, but was oftener applied to men.

Shall I argue of conversation with this *hoyden*, to go and practise at his opportunities in the larder?

Milton, *Colasterion.*

Falourdin, *m.* A bucke, lowt, lurden, a lubberly sloven, heavy sot, lumpish *hoydon.*

Cotgrave, *A French and English Dictionary.*

Badault, *m.* A fool, dolt, sot, fop, ass, coxcomb, gaping *hoydon.*

Id., *Ib.*

A rude *hoidon;* Grue, badault, falourdin, becjaune; Balordo, babionetto, rustico; Bouaron.

Howell, *Lexicon Tetraglotton.*

HUMOUR, HUMOUROUS, HUMOURIST. The four 'humours' in a man, according to the old physicians, were blood, choler, phlegm, and melancholy. So long as these were duly mixed, all would be well. But so soon as any of them unduly preponderated, the man became 'humourous,' one 'humour' or another bearing too great a sway in him. As such, his conduct would not be according to the received rule of other men, but have something peculiar, whimsical, self-willed in it. In this the self-asserting character of the 'humourous' man lay the point of contact, the middle term, between the modern use of 'humour' and the ancient. It was his 'humour' which would lead a man to take an original view and aspect of things, a 'humourous' aspect, first in the old sense, and then in that which we now employ.

In which [kingdom of heaven] neither such high-flown enthusiasts, nor any dry churlish reasoners and disputers, shall have either part or portion, till they lay down those gigantic *humours*, and become (as our Saviour Christ, who is that unerring Truth, has prescribed), like little children.

H. More, *The Grand Mystery of Godliness*, b. viii. c. 15.

Yet such is now the duke's condition,
That he misconstrues all that you have done;
The duke is *humourous*.

Shakespeare, *As you like it*, Act i. Sc. 2.

The people thereof [Ephraim] were active, valiant, ambitious of honour; but withal hasty, *humourous*, hard to be pleased; forward enough to fight with their foes, and too forward to fall out with their friends.

Fuller, *A Pisgah Sight of Palestine*, b. ii. c. 9.

Or it may be (what is little better than that), instead of the living righteousness of Christ, he will magnify himself in some *humourous* pieces of holiness of his own.

H. More, *The Grand Mystery of Godliness*, b. viii. c. 14.

The seamen are a nation by themselves, a *humourous* and fantastic people.

Clarendon, *The History of the Great Rebellion.*

Wretched men, that shake off the true comely habit of religion, to bespeak them a new-fashioned suit of profession at an *humourist's* shop!

Adams, *The Devil's Banquet*, p. 52.

I.

Idiot. A word with a very interesting and instructive history, which, however, is only fully intelligible by a reference to the Greek. The ἰδιώτης or 'idiot' is first the private man as distinguished from the man sustaining a public office; then, inasmuch as public life was considered an absolutely necessary condition of man's highest education, the untaught or mentally undeveloped, as distinguished from the educated; and only after it had run through these courses did 'idiot' come to signify what ἰδιώτης never did, the man whose mental powers are not merely unexercised but deficient, as distinguished from him in full possession of them. This is the only employment to which we now put the word; but examples of its earlier and more Greek uses are frequent in Jeremy Taylor and others.

And here, again, their allegation out of Gregory the First and Damascene, That images be the laymen's books, and that pictures are the Scripture of *idiots* and simple persons, is worthy to be considered.

Homilies; Sermon against Peril of Idolatry.

It is clear, by Bellarmine's confession, that S. Austin affirmed that the plain places of Scripture are sufficient to all laics, and all *idiots* or private persons.

J. Taylor, *A Dissuasive from Popery*, part ii. b. i. § 1.

Christ was received of *idiots*, of the vulgar people, and of the simpler sort, while He was rejected, despised, and persecuted even to death by the high priests, lawyers, scribes, doctors, and rabbies.

Blount, *Philostratus*, p. 237.

IMP. Employed in nobler senses formerly than now. 'To imp' is properly to engraft, and an 'imp' a scion or engrafted shoot; and, even as we now speak of the 'scions' of a noble house, so there was in earlier English the same natural transfer of 'imps' from plants to persons.

Of feble trees there comen wretched *impes.*

The Monkes Prologue.

The sudden taking away of those most goodly and virtuous young *imps,* the Duke of Suffolk and his brother, by the sweating sickness, was it not also a manifest token of God's heavy displeasure toward us?

Becon, *A Comfortable Epistle.*

The king returned into England with victory and triumph; the king preferred there eighty noble *imps* to the order of knighthood.

Stow, *Annals,* 1592, p. 385.

IMPOTENT, IMPOTENCE. The inner connection between weakness and violence is finely declared in Latin in the fact that 'impotens' implies both; so once did 'impotent' in English, though it now retains only the meaning of weak.

An *impotent* lover
Of women for a flash; but his fires quenched,
Hating as deadly.

Massinger, *The Unnatural Combat,* Act iii. Sc. 2.

The Lady Davey, ever *impotent* in her passions, was even distracted with anger, that she was crossed in her will.

Hacket, *The Life of Archbishop Williams,* part i. p. 194.

The truth is, that in this battle and whole business the Britons never more plainly manifested themselves to be right barbarous; such confusion, such *impotence*, as seemed likest not to a war, but to the wild hurry of a distracted woman, with as mad a crew at her heels.

Milton, *The History of England*, b. ii.

If a great personage undertakes an action passionately and upon great interest, let him manage it indiscreetly, let the whole design be unjust, let it be acted with all the malice and *impotency* in the world, he shall have enough to flatter him, but not enough to reprove him.

J. Taylor, *Holy Living*, c. 2. § 6.

INCENSE. Now to kindle *anger* only; but once to kindle or inflame any passion, good or bad, in the breast. Anger, as the strongest passion, finally appropriated the word, as in Greek it made θυμός and ὀργή its own.

He [Asdrubal] it was, that when his men were weary and drew back, *incensed* [accendit] them again, one while by fair words and entreaty, another while by sharp checks and rebukes.

Holland, *Livy*, p. 665.

Prince Edward struck his breast and swore, that though all his friends forsook him, yet he would enter Ptolemais, though only with Fowin, his horsekeeper. By which speech he *incensed* the English to go on with him.

Fuller, *The Holy War*, b. iv. c. 28.

INCIVILITY. See 'CIVIL,' 'CIVILITY.'

By this means infinite numbers of souls may be brought from their idolatry, bloody sacrifices, ignorance, and *incivility*, to the worshipping of the true God.

Sir W. Raleigh, *Of the Voyage for Guiana*.

INDIFFERENT, INDIFFERENCE, INDIFFERENTLY. It is a striking testimony of the low general average which we have come to assume common to most things, that a thing which does not *differ* from others, is thereby qualified as poor; a sentence of depreciation is pronounced upon it when it is declared to be 'indifferent.' When in Greek διαφέρειν means 'præstare,' and τὰ διαφέροντα 'præstantiora,' we have exactly the same feeling embodying itself at the other end. But this use of these words is modern. 'Indifferent' was impartial once, not *making* differences, where none really were.

God receiveth the learned and unlearned, and casteth away none, but is *indifferent* unto all.

Homilies; Exhortation to the Reading of Holy Scripture.

If overseer of the poor, he [the good parishioner] is careful the rates be made *indifferent*, whose inequality oftentimes is more burdensome than the sum.

Fuller, *The Holy State*, b. ii. c. 11.

Requesting that they might speak before the senate, and be heard with *indifference.*

Holland, *Livy*, p. 1214.

That they may truly and *indifferently* minister justice.

The Book of Common Prayer.

INDOLENCE. 'Indolentia' was a word first invented by Cicero, when he was obliged to find some equivalent for the ἀπάθεια of certain Greek schools. That it was not counted one of his happiest coinages we may conclude from the seldom use of it by any other authors but himself, as also from the fact that Seneca a little later proposed 'impatientia' as the Latin equivalent for ἀπάθεια, implying that none such had hitherto been found. The word has taken firmer root in English than it ever did in Latin; at the same time it has lost the accuracy of use which it had in the philosophical schools, where it signified a state of freedom from passion and pain, as it also did among our own writers of the Caroline period, and even later; and means now a condition of languid non-exertion.

Now, to begin with fortitude, they say it is the mean between cowardice and rash audacity, of which twain the one is a defect, the other an excess of the ireful passion; liberality between niggardise and prodigality, clemency and mildness between senseless *indolence* and cruelty.

Holland, *Plutarch's Morals*, p. 69.

Now though Christ were far from both, yet He came nearer to an excess of passion than to an *indolency*, to a senselessness, to a privation of natural affections. Inordinateness of affections may sometimes make some men like some beasts; but *indolency*, absence, emptiness, privation of affections, makes any man, at all times, like stones, like dirt.

Donne, *Sermons*, 1640, p. 156.

Indolence or *indolency*, a being insensible to pain or grief.

Phillips, *The New World of Words.*

INGENIOUS,
INGENUOUS,
INGENUITY,
INGENUOUSNESS.

We are now pretty well agreed in respect of the use of these words; but there was a time when the uttermost confusion reigned amongst them. Thus, in the first and second quotations below, 'ingenious' is used where we should now use, and where oftentimes the writers of that time would have used, 'ingenuous,' and the converse in the third; while in like manner 'ingenuity' in each of the three quotations which follow stands for our present 'ingenuousness,' and 'ingenuousness' in the last for 'ingenuity.' In respect of 'ingenious' and 'ingenuous,' the arrangement at which we have now arrived regarding their several meanings—namely, that the first indicates mental, the second moral qualities—is good; 'ingenious' being from 'ingenium,' and 'ingenuous' from 'ingenuus.' But 'ingenuity,' being from 'ingenuous,' should have kept the meaning, which it has now quite let go, of innate nobleness of disposition; while 'ingeniousness,' against which there could have been no objection to which 'ingenuousness' is not equally exposed, might have expressed what 'ingenuity' does now.

He is neither wise nor faithful, but a flatterer, that denies his spirit *ingenious* freedom.

Hacket, *The Life of Archbishop Williams,* part i. p. 150.

An *ingenious* person will rather wear a plain garment of his own than a rich livery, the mark of servitude.

Bates, *Spiritual Perfection;* Preface.

Since heaven is so glorious a state, and so certainly designed for us, if we please, let us spend all that we have, all our passions and affections, all our study and industry, all our desires and stratagems, all our witty and *ingenuous* faculties, towards the arriving thither.

J. Taylor, *Holy Dying,* c. 2, § 4.

Christian simplicity teaches openness and *ingenuity* in contracts and matters of buying and selling.

Id., *Sermon* 24, part ii.

It is the part of *ingenuity* to acknowledge by whom a man hath profited.

Oley, *Preface to Dr. Jackson's Works,* vol. i. p. 25.

It [gratitude] is such a debt as is left to every man's *ingenuity* (in respect of any legal coaction) whether he will pay it or no.

South, *Sermons*, vol. i. p. 410.

By his *ingenuousness* he [the good handicrafts-man] leaves his art better than he found it.

Fuller, *The Holy State*, b. ii. c. 19.

INSOLENT, INSOLENCE. } The 'insolent' is properly no more than the unusual. This, as the violation of the fixed law and order of society, is commonly offensive, even as it indicates a mind willing to offend; and thus 'insolent' has acquired its present meaning. But for the poet, the fact that he is forsaking the beaten track, that he can say—

"peragro loca, *nullius ante*
Trita jugo"—

in this way to be 'insolent' or original, as we should now say, may be his highest praise. The epithet 'furious' joined to 'insolence' in the second quotation is to be explained of that 'fine madness' which Spenser as a Platonist esteemed a necessary condition of the poet.

For ditty and amorous ode I find Sir Walter Raleigh's vein most lofty, *insolent*, and passionate.

Puttenham, *The Art of English Poesy*, b. i. c. 31.

Her great excellence
Lifts me above the measure of my might,
That being filled with furious *insolence*
I feel myself like one yrapt in spright.

Spenser, *Colin Clout's come home again.*

INSTITUTE, INSTITUTER, INSTITUTION. These all had once in English meanings coextensive with those of the Latin words which they represent. We now inform, instruct (the images are nearly the same), but we do not 'institute,' children any more.

A painful schoolmaster, that hath in hand
To *institute* the flower of all a land,
Gives longest lessons unto those, where Heaven
The ablest wits and aptest wills hath given.

Sylvester, *Du Bartas; Seventh Day of the First Week.*

Neither did he this for want of better instructions, having had the learnedest and wisest man reputed of all Britain, the *instituter* of his youth.

Milton, *The History of England,* b. iii.

A Short Catechism for the *institution* of young persons in the Christian Religion.

Title of a Treatise by Jeremy Taylor.

J.

JACOBIN. The great French Revolution has stamped itself too deeply and terribly upon the mind of Europe for 'Jacobin' ever again to have any other meaning than that which the famous Club, assembling in the hall of the Jacobin convent, has given it; but it needs hardly to say that a 'Jacobin' was once a Dominican friar, though this name did not extend beyond France.

Now am I young and stout and bold,
Now am I Robert, now Robin,
Now frere Minour, now *Jacobin.*

Chaucer, *The Romaunt of the Rose,* 6339.

Agent for England, send thy mistress word
What this detested *Jacobin* hath done.
Marlowe, *The Massacre at Paris*, Act iii. Sc. 4.

K.

KINDLY. Nothing ethical was connoted in 'kindly' once; it was simply the adjective of 'kind.' But it is God's ordinance that 'kind' should be 'kindly,' in our modern sense of the word as well; and thus the word has attained this meaning.

This Joon in the Gospel witnesseth that the *kyndeli* sone of God is maad man.

Wiclif, *Prologe of John.*

Forasmuch as his mind gave him, that, his nephews living, men would not reckon that he could have right to the realm, he thought therefore without delay to rid them, as though the killing of his kinsmen could amend his cause, and make him a *kindly* king.

Sir T. More, *The History of King Richard III.*

The royal eagle is called in Greek Gnesios, as one would say true and *kindly*, as descended from the gentle and right aery of eagles.

Holland, *Pliny*, vol i. p. 272.

Whatsoever as the Son of God He may do, it is *kindly* for Him as the Son of Man to save the sons of men.

Andrews, *Sermons*, vol. iv. p. 253.

KNAVE. How many serving-lads must have been unfaithful and dishonest before 'knave,' which meant at first no more than boy, acquired the meaning which it has now! Note the same history in the German 'Bube,' 'Dirne,' 'Schalk.'

If it is a *knave* child, sle ye him; if it is a womman, kepe ye.
Exodus i. 16. Wiclif.

The time is come; a *knave* childe she bare.
Chaucer, *The Man of Lawes Tale.*

O murderous slumber,
Lay'st thou thy leaden mace upon my boy,
That plays thee music? gentle *knave*, good night.
Shakespeare, *Julius Cæsar*, Act. iv. Sc. 3.

KNUCKLE. The German 'Knöchel' is any joint whatsoever; nor was our 'knuckle' limited formerly, as now it well nigh exclusively is, at least in regard of the human body, to certain smaller joints of the hand.

Thou, Nilus, wert assigned to stay her pains and travels past,
To which as soon as Io came with much ado, at last
With weary *knuckles* on thy brim she kneeled sadly down.
Golding, *Ovid's Metamorphosis*, b. i.

But when
"his scornful muse could ne'er abide
With tragic shoes her *ancles* for to hide"—
the pace of the verse told me that her maukin *knuckles* were never shapen to that royal buskin.
Milton, *Apology for Smectymnuus*, p. 186.

L.

LACE. That which now commonly bears this name has it on the score of its curiously-woven threads;

but 'lace,' probably identical with the Latin 'lacqueus,' though it has not reached *us* through the Latin, being the same word, only differently spelt, as 'latch,' is mostly used by our earlier writers in the more proper sense of a snare.

> And in my mind I measure pace by pace,
> To seek the place where I myself had lost,
> That day that I was tangled in the *lace*
> In seeming slack, that knitteth ever most.
>
> Surrey, *The Restless State of a Lover*.

> Yet if the polype can get and entangle him [the lobster] once within his long *laces*, he dies for it.
>
> Holland, *Plutarch's Morals*, p. 973.

LANDSCAPE. The second syllable in 'land*scape*' or 'land*skip*' is only a solitary example of an earlier form of the same termination which we meet in 'friend*ship*,' 'lord*ship*,' 'fellow*ship*,' and the like. As these mean the manner or fashion of a friend, of a lord, and so on, so 'landscape' the manner or fashion of the land; and in our earlier English this rather as the pictured or otherwise imitated model, than in its very self. As this imitation would be necessarily in small, the word acquired the secondary meaning of a compendium or multum in parvo ; cf. Skinner, *Etymologicon*, s. v. *Landskip:* Tabula chorographica, primario autem terra, provincia, seu topographica σκιαγραφία.

> The sins of other women show in *landskip*, far off and full of shadow; hers [a harlot's] *in statue*, near hand and bigger in the life.
>
> Sir Thomas Overbury, *Characters*.

London, as you know, is our Ἑλλάδος Ἑλλάς, our England of England, and our *landskip* and representation of the whole island.

Hacket, *The Life of Archbishop Williams*, part ii. p. 59.

That detestable traitor, that prodigy of nature, that opprobrium of mankind, that *landscape* of iniquity, that sink of sin, and that compendium of baseness, who now calls himself our Protector.

An Address sent by the Anabaptists to the King, 1658, in Clarendon, *The History of the Great Rebellion*, b. xv.

LATCH. Few things now are 'latched' or caught except a door or casement; but the word, being the same as 'to lace,' was once of much wider use.

Those that remained threw darts at our men, and *latching* our darts, sent them again at us.

Golding, *Cæsar*, p. 60.

Peahens are wont to lay by night, and that from an high place where they perch; and then, unless there be good heed taken that the eggs be *latched* in some soft bed underneath, they are soon broken.

Holland, *Pliny*, vol. i. p. 301.

LEVY. Troops are now raised, or 'levied,' indifferently; but a siege is only raised, and not 'levied,' as it, too, once might have been.

Euphranor having *levied* the siege from this one city, forthwith led his army to Demetrias.

Holland, *Livy*, p. 1178.

LEWD, LEWDNESS. There are three distinct stages in the meaning of the word 'lewd;' of these it has entirely overlived two, and survives only in the third, namely, in that of wanton or lascivious. Without discussing here its etymology or its exact relation to 'lay,' it is sufficient to observe, that, as 'lay,' it was often used in the sense of ignorant, or rather unlearned. Next, according to the proud saying of the Pharisees, "This people who knoweth not the law are cursed" (*John* vii. 49), and on the assumption, which would have its truth, that those untaught in the doctrines, would be unexercised in the practices, of Christianity, it came to signify vicious, though without designating one vice more than others. While in its present and third stage, it has, like so many other words, retired from this general designation of all vices, to express one of the more frequent, alone.

> Archa Dei in the olde law Levytes it kepte;
> Had never *lewed* men leve to leggen honde on that cheste.
>
> *Piers Ploughman,* 7668.

> For as moche as the curatis ben often so *lewed,* that thei understonden not bookis of Latyn for to teche the peple, it is spedful not only to the *lewed* peple, but also to the *lewed* curatis, to have bookis in Englisch of needful loore to the *lewed* peple.
>
> *Wycliffe Mss.,* p. 5.

> Of sondry doutes thus they jangle and trete,
> As *lewed* people demen comunly
> Of thinges that ben made more subtilly
> Than they can in hir *lewednesse* comprehend.
>
> Chaucer, *The Squieres Tale.*

> Neither was it Christ's intention that there should be any thing in it [the Lord's Prayer] dark or far from our capacity, specially since it belongeth equally to all, and is as necessary for the *lewd* as the learned.
>
> *A Short Catechism,* 1553.

If it were a matter of wrong or wicked *lewdness* [ῥᾳδιούργημα], O ye Jews, reason would that I should bear with you.

Acts xviii. 14. Authorized Version.

Libertine. A striking evidence of the extreme likelihood that he who has no restraints on his belief will ere long have none upon his life, is given by this word 'libertine.' Applied at first to certain heretical sects, and intended to mark the licentious *liberty* of their creed, 'libertine' soon let go altogether its relation to what a man believed, and acquired the sense which it now has, a 'libertine' being one who has released himself from all moral restraints, and especially in his relations with the other sex.

That the Scriptures do not contain in them all things necessary to salvation, is the fountain of many great and capital errors; I instance in the whole doctrine of the *libertines*, familists, quakers, and other enthusiasts, which issue from this corrupted fountain.

J. Taylor, *A Dissuasive from Popery*, part ii. b. 1. § 2.

It is not to be denied that the said *libertine* doctrines do more contradict the doctrine of the Gospel, even Christianity itself, than the doctrines of the Papists about the same subjects do.

Baxter, *Catholic Theology*, part iii. p. 289.

It is too probable that our modern *libertines*, deists, and atheists, took occasion from the scandalous contentions of Christians about many things, to disbelieve all.

A Discourse of Logomachies, 1711.

Litigious. This word has changed from an objective to a subjective sense. Things were 'litigious' once, which offered matter of litigation; persons are 'litigious' now, who are prone to litigation. Both meanings are to be found in the Latin 'litigiosus,' though predominantly that which we have now made the sole meaning.

Dolopia he hath subdued by force of arms, and could not abide to hear that the determination of certain provinces, which were debatable and *litigious*, should be referred to the award of the people of Rome.

Holland, *Livy*, p. 1111.

Of the articles gainsaid by a great outcry, three and no more did seem to be *litigious*.

Hacket, *The Life of Archbishop Williams*, part i. p. 140.

No fences parted fields, nor marks nor bounds
Distinguished acres of *litigious* grounds.

Dryden, *Virgil's Georgics*, b. i. 193, 4.

LIVELY. This was once nearly, if not altogether, equipollent with 'living.' We have here the explanation of a circumstance which many probably have noted and regretted in the Authorized Version of the New Testament, namely, that while λίθον ζῶντα at 1 *Pet.* ii. 4 is 'a *living* stone,' λίθοι ζῶντες, which follows immediately, ver. 5, is only '*lively* stones,' 'living' being thus brought down to 'lively,' with no correspondent reduction in the original to warrant it. But when our Version was made, there was scarcely any distinction between the forces of the words. Still it would certainly have been better to adhere to one word or the other.

Was it well done to suffer him, imprisoned in chains, lying in a dark dungeon, to draw his *lively* breath at the pleasure of the hangman?

Holland, *Livy*, p. 228.

Had I but seen thy picture in this plight,
It would have madded me; what shall I do
Now I behold thy *lively* body so?
Shakespeare, *Titus Andronicus*, Act iii. Sc. 1.

That his dear father might interment have,
See, the young man entered a *lively* grave.
Massinger, *The Fatal Dowry*, Act ii. Sc. 1.

LIVERY. It need hardly be observed that the explanation of 'livery' which Spenser offers (see below), is perfectly correct; but we do not any longer recognize the second of those uses of the word there mentioned by him. It is no longer applied to the ration, or stated portion of food, delivered at stated periods (the σιτομέτριον of *Luke* xii. 42), either to the members of a household, to soldiers, or to others.

What *livery* is, we by common use in England know well enough, namely, that is, allowance of horse-meat, as to keep horses at *livery*, the which word, I guess, is derived of livering or delivering forth their nightly food. So in great houses the *livery* is said to be served up for all night. And *livery* is also the upper weed which a servant-man weareth, so called, as I suppose, for that it was delivered and taken from him at pleasure.

Spenser, *View of the State of Ireland.*

The emperor's officers every night went through the town from house to house, whereat any English gentleman did repast or lodge, and served their *liveries* for all night; first the officers brought into the house a cast of fine manchet, and of silver two great pots, with white wine, and sugar, to the weight of a pound, &c.

Cavendish, *The Life of Cardinal Wolsey*.

LUCID INTERVAL. We limit this at present to the brief and transient season when a mind, ordinarily clouded and obscured by insanity, recovers for a while its clearness. It had no such limitation formerly, but was of very wide use, as the four passages quoted below, in each of which its application is different, will show.

East of Edom lay the land of Uz, where Job dwelt, so renowned for his patience, when the devil heaped afflictions upon him, allowing him no *lucid intervals.*

Fuller, *A Pisgah Sight of Palestine,* b. iv. c. 2.

Some beams of wit on other souls may fall,
Strike through, and make a *lucid interval:*
But Shadwell's genuine night admits no ray,
His rising fogs prevail upon the day.

Dryden, *Mac-Flecknoe.*

Such is the nature of man, that it requires *lucid intervals;* and the vigour of the mind would flag and decay, should it always jog on at the rate of a common enjoyment, without being sometimes quickened and exalted with the vicissitude of some more refined pleasure.

South, *Sermons,* 1744, vol. viii. p. 403.

Thus he [Lord Lyttleton] continued, giving his dying benediction to all around him. On Monday morning a *lucid interval* gave some small hopes; but these vanished in the evening.

Narrative of the Physician, inserted in Johnson's Life of Lord Lyttleton.

Lumber. As the Lombards were the bankers, so also they were the pawnbrokers of the middle ages; indeed, as they would often advance money upon pledges, the two businesses were very closely joined, would often run in, to one another. The 'lumber' room was originally the Lombard room, or room where the Lombard banker and broker stored his pledges; 'lumber' then, as in the passage from Butler, the pawns and pledges themselves. As these would naturally often accumulate here till they became out of date and unserviceable, the steps are easy to be traced by which the word came to possess its present meaning.

Lumber, potius *lumbar*, as to put one's clothes to *lumbar*, *i. e.* pignori dare, oppignorare.

Skinner, *Etymologicon.*

And by an action falsely laid of trover
The *lumber* for their proper goods recover.

Butler, *Upon Critics.*

They put up all the little plate they had in the *lumber*, which is pawning it, till the ships came.

Lady Murray, *Lives of George Baillie and of Lady Grisell Baillie.*

LURCH. 'To lurch' is seldom used now except of a ship, which 'lurches' when it makes something of a headlong dip in the sea; the fact that by so doing it, partially at least, hides itself, and so 'lurks,' for 'lurk' and 'lurch' are identical, explains this employment of the word. But 'to lurch,' generally as an active verb, was of much more frequent use in early English; and soon superinduced on the sense of lying concealed that of lying in wait with the view of intercepting and seizing a prey. After a while this superadded notion of intercepting and seizing some booty quite thrust out that of lying concealed; as in all three of the quotations which follow.

It is not an auspicate beginning of a feast, nor agreeable to amity and good fellowship, to snatch or *lurch* one from another, to have many hands in a dish at once, striving a vie who should be more nimble with his fingers.

Holland, *Plutarch's Morals*, p. 679.

I speak not of many more [discommodities of a residence]; too far off from great cities, which may hinder business; or too near them, which *lurcheth* all provisions, and maketh every thing dear.

Bacon, *Essays*, 45.

At the beginning of this war [the Crusades] the Pope's temporal power in Italy was very slender; but soon after he grew within short time without all measure, and did *lurch* a castle here, gain a city there from the emperor, while he was employed in Palestine.

Fuller, *The Holy War*, b. i. c. 11.

LUXURY, LUXURIOUS. 'Luxuria' in classical Latin was very much what our 'luxury' is now. The meaning which in our earlier English was its only one, namely, indulgence in sins of the flesh, is derived from its use in the medieval ethics, where it never means anything else but this. The weakening of the influence of the scholastic theology, joined to a nearer acquaintance with classical Latinity, has probably caused its return to the classical meaning. In the definition given by Phillips (see below), the word may be noticed in the process of transition from its old meaning to its new, the old still remaining, but the new superinduced upon it.

O foule lust of *luxurie*, to thin ende
Not only that thou taintest mannes mind,
But veraily thou wolt his body shende.

Chaucer, *The Man of Lawes Tale.*

Luxury and lust fasten a rust and foulness on the mind, that it cannot see sin in its odious deformity, nor virtue in its unattainable beauty.

Bates, *Spiritual Perfection*, c. 1.

Luxury, all superfluity and excess in carnal pleasures, sumptuous fare or building; sensuality, riotousness, profuseness.

Phillips, *The New World of Words.*

She knows the heat of a *luxurious* bed.

Shakespeare, *Much Ado about Nothing*, Act iv. Sc. 1.

Again, that many of their Popes be such as I have said, naughty, wicked, *luxurious* men, they openly confess.

Jackson, *The Eternal Truth of Scriptures*, b. ii. c. 14.

M.

MAGNIFICENT, MAGNIFICENCE. } Frequently used by our elder writers where we should employ munificent or generous. In their employment of the word, as well as in ours, lies the notion of cost and large outlay, only in theirs this as bestowed by men upon others, in ours on themselves. There lay behind both uses an earlier and a nobler than either, as is evident from my first quotation.

Then cometh *magnificence*, that is to say when a man doth and performeth gret werkes of goodnesse.

Chaucer, *The Persones Tale.*

Every amorous person becometh liberal and *magnificent*, although he had been aforetime a pinching snudge; in such sort as men take more pleasure to give away and bestow upon those whom they love, than they do to take and receive of others.

Holland, *Plutarch's Morals*, p. 1147.

Am I close-handed,
Because I scatter not among you that
I must not call my own? know, you court-leeches,
A prince is never so *magnificent*
As when he's sparing to enrich a few
With the injuries of many.
Massinger, *The Emperor of the East*, Act ii. Sc. 1.

Bounty and *magnificence* are virtues very regal; but a prodigal king is nearer a tyrant than a parsimonious.
Bacon, *Essays, Of a King.*

MAKE, MAKER. } It would be curious to determine whether 'maker,' as equivalent to poet, and 'to make' as applied to the exercise of the poet's art, are words of genuine home-growth, or mere imitations of the Greek ποιητής and ποιεῖν, a point which Sir P. Sidney, as will be seen below, declines to determine. There are so many words and in so many languages which mark men's sense that invention, and in a certain sense creation, is the essential character of the poet, such as the Saxon 'song-smith,' the French 'trouvère,' 'troubadour,' that one might be almost tempted to think of the words not as introduced from without, but as a spontaneous birth of our own tongue. At the same time it must be owned as against this is the fact, that the words are not found in any book anterior to the revival of the study of the Greek literature and language in England; and Sir J. Harrington affirms (*Apology of Poetry*, p. 2), though in this he is certainly mistaken, that Puttenham in his *Art of English Poesy*, 1589, was the first who gave 'make' and 'maker' this meaning.

> The God of shepherds, Tityrus, is dead,
> Who taught me, homely as I can, to *make*.
>
> Spenser, *The Shepherd's Calendar, June.*

The old famous poet Chaucer, whom for his excellency and wonderful skill in *making*, his scholar Lidgate (a worthy scholar of so excellent a master) calleth the lode-star of our language.

E. K., *Epistle Dedicatory to Spenser's Shepherd's Calendar.*

There cannot be in a *maker* a fouler fault than to falsify his accent to serve his cadence, or by untrue orthography to wrench his words to help his rhyme.

Puttenham, *The Art of English Poesy*, b. ii. c. 8.

The Greeks named the poet ποιητής, which name, as the most excellent, hath gone through other languages. It cometh of this word ποιεῖν, to make; wherein I know not whether by luck or wisdom we Englishmen have met well with the Greeks in calling him a *maker*.

Sir P. Sidney, *The Defence of Poetry.*

MANURE. This is the same word as 'manœuvre,' to work with the hand; and thus, to till or cultivate the earth; this tillage being in earlier periods of society the great and predominant labor of the hands. We restrain the word now to one particular branch of this cultivation, but our ancestors made it to embrace the whole.

It [Japan] is mountainous and craggy, full of rocks and stony places, so that the third part of this empire is not inhabited or *manured*

Memorials of Japan (Hackluyt Society), p. 3.

A rare and excellent wit untaught doth bring forth many good and evil things together; as a fat soil, that lieth *unmanured*, bringeth forth both herbs and weeds.

North, *Plutarch's Lives*, p. 185.

Every man's hand itching to throw a cudgel at him, who, like a nut-tree, must be *manured* by beating, or else would never bear fruit.

Fuller, *The Holy War*, b. ii. c. 11.

Measles. This has only been by later use restrained to one kind of *spotted* sickness; but 'meazel' (it is spelt in innumerable ways) was once leprosy, or more often the leper himself, and the disease, 'meselry.'

Forsothe he was a stronge man and riche, but *mesell*.

4 *Kings* v. 1. Wiclif.

In this same year the *mysseles* thorow oute Cristendom were slaundered that thei had mad covenaunt with Sarasenes for to poison all Christen men.

Capgrave, *Chronicle of England*, p. 186.

He [Pope Deodatus] kissed a *mysel*, and sodeynly the *mysel* was whole.

Id., *Ib.*, p. 95.

Mechanical. This now simply expresses a fact, and is altogether untinged with passion or sentiment; but in its early history it ran exactly parallel to the Greek βάναυσος, which, expressing first the sitting by the stove, as one plying a handicraft might do, came afterward, in obedience to certain constant tendencies of language, to imply the man ethically illiberal.

Base and *mechanical* niggardise they [flatterers] account temperate frugality.

Holland, *Plutarch's Morals*, p. 93.

Base dunghill villain, and *mechanical.*

Shakespeare, 2 *Henry VI.* Act i. Sc. 3.

It was never a good world, since employment was counted *mechanick,* and idleness gentility.

Whitlock, *Zootomia,* p. 30.

MEDDLE. This had once no such offensive meaning of mixing oneself up in other people's business, as now it has. On the contrary, Barrow in one of his sermons draws expressly the distinction between 'meddling' and being meddlesome, and only condemns the latter.

In the drynke that she *meddlid* to you, mynge ye double to her.

Apoc. xviii. 6. Wiclif.

How is it that thou, being a Jew, askest drink of me, which am a Samaritan? For the Jews *meddle* not [οὐ συγχρῶνται] with the Samaritans.

John iv. 9. Cranmer.

We beseech you, brethren, that ye study to be quiet, and to *meddle* with your own business.

1 *Thess.* iv. 10, 11. Tyndale.

Tho he, that had well y-conned his lere,
Thus *medled* his talk with many a tear.

Spenser, *The Shepherd's Calendar, May.*

MEDITERRANEAN. Only seas are 'mediterranean' now, and indeed we may say, only one Sea; but there is no reason why cities and countries should not be characterized as 'mediterranean' as well. We have preferred, however, to employ 'inland.'

An old man, full of days, and living still in your *mediterranean* city, Coventry.

Henry Holland, *Preface to Holland's Cyropædia.*

It [Arabia] hath store of cities as well *mediterranean* as maritime.

Holland, *Ammianus.*

Medley. It is plain from the frequent use of the French 'mêlée' in the description of battles that we feel the want of a parallel English word. There have even been attempts, though hardly successful ones, to naturalize 'mêlée,' and as 'volée' has become in English 'volley,' that so 'mêlée' should become 'melley.' Perhaps, as Tennyson has sanctioned these, employing 'mellay' in his *Princess*, they may now succeed. But there would have been no need of this, nor yet of borrowing a foreign word, if 'medley' had been allowed to keep this more passionate use, which once it possessed.

The consul for his part forslowed not to come to hand-fight. The *medley* continued above three hours, and the hope of victory hung in equal balance.

Holland, *Livy*, p. 1119.

Melancholy. This has now ceased, nearly or altogether, to designate a particular form of moody madness, the German 'Tiefsinn,' which was ascribed by the old physicians to a predominance of *black bile* mingling with the blood. It was not, it is true, always restrained to this peculiar form of mental unsoundness; thus, Burton's 'Anatomy of *Melancholy*' has not to do with this one form of madness, but with all. This, however, was its prevailing use, and here is to be found the link of connection between its present use, as a deep pensiveness or sadness, and its past.

That property of *melancholy*, whereby men become to be delirous in some one point, their judgment standing untouched in others.

H. More, *A brief Discourse of Enthusiasm*, sect. 14.

Luther's conference with the devil might be, for ought I know, nothing but a *melancholy* dream.

Chillingworth, *The Religion of Protestants, Preface.*

Though I am persuaded that none but the devil and this *melancholy* miscreant were in the plot [the Duke of Buckingham's murder], yet in foro Dei many were guilty of this blood, that rejoiced it was spilt.

Hacket, *The Life of Archbishop Williams*, part ii. p. 80.

Some *melancholy* men have believed that elephants and birds and other creatures have a language whereby they discourse with one another.

Bishop Reynolds, *The Passions and Faculties of the Soul of Man*, c. 39.

MERE, MERELY. There is a good note on these words, and on the changes of meaning which they have undergone, in Craik's *English of Shakespeare*, p. 80. He there says: "Merely (from the Latin merus and mere) means purely, only. It separates that which it designates and qualifies from every thing else. But in so doing the chief or most emphatic reference may be made either to that which is included, or to that which is excluded. In modern English it is always to the latter. In Shakespeare's day the other reference was more common, that, namely, to what was included."

Our wine is here mingled with water and with myrrh; there [in the life to come] it is *mere* and unmixed.

J. Taylor, *The Worthy Communicant.*

The great winding-sheets, that bury all things in oblivion, are two, deluges and earthquakes. As for conflagrations and great droughts, they do not *merely* dispeople and* destroy. Phaethon's car went but a day; and the three years' drought, in the time of Elias, was but particular, and left people alive.

Bacon, *Essays*, 58.

Fye on't! O fye! 'tis an unweeded garden,
That grows to seed; things rank and gross in nature
Possess it *merely*.

Shakespeare, *Hamlet.* Act i. Sc. 2.

Mess. This used continually to be applied to a quaternion, or group of *four* persons or things. Probably in the distribution of food to large numbers, it was found most convenient to arrange them in *fours*, and hence this application of the word.

Where are your *mess*† of sons to back you now?

Shakespeare, 3 *Henry VI.* Act i. Sc. 4.

There lacks a fourth thing to make up the *mess*.

Latimer, *Sermon* 5.

Metal. The Latin 'metallum' signified a mine before it signified the metal which was found in the mine; and Jeremy Taylor uses 'metal' in this sense of mine. I am not certain whether this may not be a latinism peculiar to him, as he has of such not a

* A recent editor of Bacon, I need hardly say not the *most* recent, has made a hopeless confusion by changing the 'and' into 'but,' evidently from not understanding the old use of 'merely.'

† Edward, George, Richard, and Edmund.

few; in which case it would scarcely have a right to a place in this little volume, which does not propose to note the peculiarities of single writers, but the general course of the language. I, however, insert it, counting it more probable that my limited reading hinders me from furnishing an example of this use from some other author, than that such does not somewhere exist.

It was impossible to live without our king, but as slaves live, that is, such who are civilly dead, and persons condemned to *metals.*
J. Taylor, *Ductor Dubitantium, Epistle Dedicatory.*

METHODIST. This term is restricted at present to the followers of John Wesley; but it was once applied to those who followed a certain 'method' in philosophical speculation, or in the ethical treatment of themselves or others.

The finest *methodists,* according to Aristotle's golden rule of artificial bounds, condemn geometrical precepts in arithmetic, or arithmetical precepts in geometry, as irregular and abusive.
G. Harvey, *Pierce's Supererogation,* p. 117.

All of us have some or other tender parts of our souls, which we cannot endure should be ungently touched; every man must be his own *methodist* to find them out.
Jackson, *Justifying Faith,* b. iv. c. 5.

MINUTE. 'Minutes' are now 'minúte' portions of time; they might once be 'minúte' portions of any thing. 'Mite,' as the quotation from Wiclif plainly shows, is contracted from 'minute,' being a 'minute' portion of money.

But whanne a pore widewe was come, sche cast two *mynutis*, that is a ferthing.

Mark xii. 42. Wiclif.

Let us, with the poor widow of the Gospel, at least give two *minutes*.

Becon, *The Nosegay, Preface.*

And now, after such a sublimity of malice, I will not instance in the sacrilegious ruin of the neighbouring temples, which needs must have perished in the flame. These are but *minutes*, in respect of the ruin prepared for the living temples.

J. Taylor, *Sermon on the Gunpowder Treason.*

Miscreant. A settled conviction that to believe wrongly is the way to live wrongly has caused that in all languages words, which originally did but indicate the first, have gradually acquired a meaning of the second. There is no more illustrious example of this than 'miscreant,' which now charges him to whom it is applied not with religious error, but with extreme moral depravity; while yet, according to its etymology, it did but mean at the first misbeliever, and as such would have been as freely applied to the morally most blameless of these as to the vilest and the worst. In the quotation from Shakespeare, York means to charge the Maid of Orleans, as a dealer in unlawful charms, with apostasy from the Christian faith, according to the low and unworthy estimate of her character, above which even Shakespeare himself has not risen.

We are not therefore ashamed of the Gospel of our Lord Jesus Christ, because *miscreants* in scorn have upbraided us that the highest of our wisdom is, Believe.

Hooker, *Ecclesiastical Polity*, b. v.

Curse, *miscreant*, when thou comest to the stake.

Shakespeare, 1 *Henry VI.* Act v. Sc. 2.

The consort and the principal servants of Soliman had been honourably restored without ransom; and the emperor's generosity to the *miscreant* was interpreted as treason to the Christian cause.

Gibbon, *The Decline and Fall of the Roman Empire*, c. 58.

MISER, MISERY, MISERABLE. We may notice a curious shifting of parts in the words 'miser,' 'misery,' 'miserable.' There was a time when the 'miser' was the wretched man, he is now the covetous; at the same time 'misery,' which is now wretchedness, and 'miserable,' which is now wretched, were severally covetousness and covetous. They have in fact exactly reversed their uses. Men still express by some words of this group, although not by the same, by 'miser' (and 'miserly'), not as once by 'misery' and 'miserable,' their deep moral conviction that the avaricious man is his own tormentor, and bears his punishment involved in his sin. I may mention here that a passage, too long to quote, in Gascoigne's *Fruits of War*, st. 72–74, is very instructive on the different uses of the word 'miser' even in his time, and on the manner in which it was even then hovering between the two meanings.

Because thou sayest, That I am rich and enriched and lack nothing; and knowest not that thou art a *miser* [et nescis quia tu es *miser*, Vulg.] and miserable and poor and blind and naked.

Rev. iii. 17. Rheims.

Vouchsafe to stay your steed for humble *miser's* sake.

Spenser, *The Fairy Queen*, ii. 1, 8.

He [Perseus] returned again to his old humour which was born and bred with him, and that was avarice and *misery*.

North, *Plutarch's Lives*, p. 215.

But Brutus, scorning his [Octavius Cæsar's] *misery* and niggardliness, gave unto every band a number of wethers to sacrifice, and fifty silver drachmas to every soldier.

Id., *Ib.* p. 830.

If avarice be thy vice, yet make it not thy punishment; *miserable* men commiserate not themselves; bowelless unto themselves, and merciless unto their own bowels.

Sir T. Browne, *Letter to a Friend.*

The liberal-hearted man is by the opinion of the prodigal, *miserable;* and by the judgment of the *miserable*, lavish.

Hooker, *Ecclesiastical Polity*, b. v. c. 65.

MISS. Now to be conscious of the loss of, nearly answers to the Latin 'desiderare,' but once to do without, to dispense with.

But as 'tis,
We cannot *miss* him; he does make our fire,
Fetch in our wood, and serves in offices
That profit us.

Shakespeare, *The Tempest*, Act i. Sc. 2.

I will have honest valiant souls about me:
I cannot *miss* thee.

Beaumont and Fletcher, *The Mad Lover*, Act ii.

MODEL. It needs hardly to be observed that 'model' is 'module,' or 'modulus,' a diminutive of 'modus;'

but this diminutive sense which once went constantly with the word, and which will alone explain the quotations which follow, when it lies in the word now, lies in it only by accident.

> O England, *model* to thy inward greatness,
> Like little body with a mighty heart.
>
> Shakespeare, *Henry V.*, Act ii. Chorus.

> And nothing can we call our own but death,
> And that small *model* of the barren earth
> Which serves as paste and cover to our bones.
>
> Id., *Richard II.*, Act iii. Sc. 2.

If Solomon's Temple were compared to some structures and fanes of heathen gods, it would appear as St. Gregory's to St. Paul's (the babe by the mother's side), or rather this David's *model* would be like David himself standing by Goliath, so gigantic were some pagan fabrics in comparison thereof.

Fuller, *A Pisgah Sight of Palestine*, b. iii. c. 3.

MOUNTEBANK. Now *any* antic fool; but once restrained to the quack-doctor who at fairs and such places of resort having *mounted* on a *bank* or *bench*, from thence proclaimed the virtue of his drugs: "a fellow above the vulgar more by three planks and two empty hogsheads than by any true skill" (Whitlock, *Zootomia*, p. 436).

Much like to these *mount-bank* chirurgians, who for to have the greater practice make show of their cunning casts and operations of their art in public theatres.

Holland, *Plutarch's Morals*, p. 111.

Such is the weakness and easy credulity of men, that a *mountebank* or cunning woman is preferred before an able physician.

Whitlock, *Zootomia*, p. 437.

Above the reach of antidotes, the power
Of the famed Pontic *mountebank* to cure.
Oldham, *Third Satire upon the Jesuits.*

Mutton. It is a refinement in the English language, one wanting in some other languages which count themselves as refined or more, that it has in so many cases one word to express the living animal, and another its flesh prepared for food; ox and beef, calf and veal, deer and venison, sheep and mutton. In respect of this last pair the refinement is of somewhat late introduction. At one time they were mere synonyms.

Peucestas, having feasted them in the kingdom of Persia, and given every soldier a *mutton* to sacrifice, thought he had won great favor and credit among them.
North, *Plutarch's Lives*, p. 505.

A starved *mutton's* carcass would better fit their palates.
B. Jonson, *The Sad Shepherd*, Act i. Sc. 2.

N.

Namely. Now only designates; but, like the German 'namentlich,' once designated as first and chief, as above all.

Sir Richard Ratclife and Sir William Catesby, which, longing for no more partners of the prince's favour, and *namely* not for him [Sir James Tyrell], whose pride they wist would bear no peer, kept him by secret drifts out of all secret trust.
Sir T. More, *The History of King Richard III.*

For there are many disobedient, and talkers of vanity, and deceivers of minds, *namely* [μάλιστα] they of the circumcision.

Tit. i. 10. Tyndale.

For in the darkness occasioned by the opposition of the earth just in the mids between the sun and the moon, there was nothing for him [Nicias] to fear, and *namely* at such a time, when there was cause for him to have stood upon his feet, and served valiantly in the field.

Holland, *Plutarch's Morals*, p. 265.

Naturalist. He is at present the scientific student of nature; but in the sixteenth and seventeenth centuries the name was often given to the deist, as one who denied Revelation and any but a religion *of nature*. "Natural religion men" such were sometimes called.

But that he [the atheist] might not be shy of me, I have conformed myself as near his own garb as I might, without partaking of his folly or wickedness; and have appeared in the plain shape of a mere *naturalist* myself, that I might, if it were possible, win him off from downright atheism.

H. More, *An Antidote against Atheism*, Preface, p. 7.

This is the invention of Satan, that whereas all will not be profane, nor *naturalists*, nor epicures, but will be religious, lo, he hath a bait for every fish, and can insinuate himself as well into religion itself as into lusts and pleasures.

Rogers, *Naaman the Syrian*, p. 115.

Heathen *naturalists* hold better consort with the primitive Church concerning the nature of sin original than the Socinians.

Jackson, *A Treatise of Christ's Everlasting Priesthood*, b. x. c. 8. § 4.

Nephew. Restrained in our present use to the son of a brother or a sister; but formerly of much laxer use, a grandson, or even a remoter lineal descendant. 'Nephew' in fact has undergone exactly the same change of meaning that 'nepos' in Latin underwent; which in the Augustan age meaning grandson, in the post-Augustan acquired the signification of 'nephew' in our present acceptation of that word.

The warts, black moles, spots and freckles of fathers, not appearing at all upon their own children's skin, begin afterwards to put forth and show themselves in their *nephews,* to wit, the children of their sons and daughters.

Holland, *Plutarch's Morals*, p. 555.

With what intent they [the apocryphal books] were first published, those words of the *nephew* of Jesus do plainly enough signify: After that my *grandfather* Jesus had given himself to the reading of the law and the prophets, he purposed also to write something pertaining to learning and wisdom.

Hooker, *Ecclesiastical Polity*, b. v. c. 20.

If any widow have children or *nephews* [ἔκγονα], let them learn first to show piety at home, and to requite their parents.

1 *Tim.* v. 4. Authorized Version.

NICE. The use of 'nice' in the sense of fastidious, difficult to please, still survives, indeed this is now, as in times past, the ruling notion of the word; only this 'niceness' is taken now much oftener in good part than in ill; nor, even when taken in an ill sense, would the word be used exactly as in the passage which follows.

A. W. [Antony a Wood] was with him several times, ate and drank with him, and had several discourses with him concerning arms and armory, which he understood well; but he found him *nice* and supercilious.

Anthony a Wood, *Athenæ Oxonienses,* 1848, vol. i. p. 161.

NIECE. This word has undergone the same change and limitation of meaning as 'nephew' *(q. v.)* with indeed the further limitation that it is now applied to the female sex alone, to the daughter of a brother or a sister, being once used, as 'neptis' was at the first, for children's children, male and female alike.

Laban answeride to hym: My dowytres and sones, and the flockis, and alle that thou beholdist, ben myne, and what may I do to my sones and to my *neces?*

Gen. xxxi. 43; cf. *Exod.* xxxiv. 7. Wiclif.

The Emperor Augustus, among other singularities that he had by himself during his life, saw, ere he died, the nephew of his *niece,* that is to say his progeny to the fourth degree of lineal descent.

Holland, *Pliny,* vol. i. p. 162.

Within the compass of which very same time he [Julius Cæsar] lost by death first his mother, then his daughter Julia, and not long after his *niece* by the said daughter.

Id., *Suetonius,* p. 11.

NOISOME. At present offensive and moving disgust; but once noxious and actually hurtful. In all passages of the Authorized Translation of the Bible where the word occurs, it is used not in its present meaning, but its past.

They that will be rich fall into temptations and snares, and into many foolish and *noisome* [βλαβεράς] lusts, which drown men in perdition and destruction.

1 *Tim.* vi. 9. Geneva.

He [the superstitious person] is persuaded that they be gods indeed, but such as be *noisome*, hurtful, and doing mischief unto men.

Holland, *Plutarch's Morals*, p. 260.

They [the prelates] are so far from hindering dissension, that they have made unprofitable, and even *noisome*, the chiefest remedy we have to keep Christendom at one, which is, by Councils.

Milton, *The Reason of Church Government*, b. i. c. 6.

Novelist. He now is, or ought to be, the writer of new tales; he was once an innovator, a bringer-in of new fashions into the Church or State.

But, see and say what you will, *novelists* had rather be talked of, that they began a fashion and set a copy for others, than to keep within the imitation of the most excellent precedents.

Hacket, *The Life of Archbishop Williams*, part ii. p. 36.

Every *novelist* with a whirligig in his brain must broach new opinions, and those made canons, nay sanctions, as sure as if a General Council had confirmed them.

Adams, *The Devil's Banquet*, 1614, p. 52.

Nursery. We have but one use of 'nursery' at this present, namely, as the place of nursing; but it was once applied as well to the person nursed, or the act of nursing.

A jolly dame, no doubt; as appears by the well battling of the plump boy, her *nursery*.

Fuller, *A Pisgah Sight of Palestine*, part i. b. ii. c. 8.

If *nursery* exceeds her [a mother's] strength, and yet her conscience will scarce permit her to lay aside and free herself from so natural, so religious a work, yet tell her, God loves mercy better than sacrifice.

Rogers, *Matrimonial Honour*, p. 247.

O.

OBELISK. The 'obelus' is properly a sharp-pointed spear or spit; with a sign resembling this, spurious or doubtful passages were marked in the books of antiquity, which sign bore therefore this name of 'obelus,' or sometimes of its diminutive 'obeliscus.' It is in this sense that we find 'obelisk' employed by the writers in the seventeenth century; while for us at the present a small pillar tapering toward the summit is the only 'obelisk' that we know.

The Lord Keeper, the most circumspect of any man alive to provide for uniformity, and to countenance it, was scratched with their *obelisk*, that he favoured Puritans, and that sundry of them had protection through his connivency or clemency.

Hacket, *The Life of Archbishop Williams*, part i. p. 95.

I have set my mark upon them [*i. e.* affected pedantic words]; and if any of them may have chanced to escape the *obelisk*, there can arise no other inconvenience from it but an occasion to exercise the choice and judgment of the reader.

Phillips, *The New World of Words*, Preface.

OBNOXIOUS. In its present lax and slovenly use, a vague unserviceable synonym for offensive, it is properly applied to one who on the ground of a mischief or wrong committed by him is justly liable to punishment (*ob noxam* pœnæ obligatus); and is used in this sense by South (see below). But there often falls out of the word the sense of a wrong committed; and that of liability to punishment, whether just or unjust, only remains; it does so very markedly in the quotation from Donne. But we punish or wish to punish those whom we dislike, and thus 'obnoxious' had obtained its present sense of offensive.

They envy Christ, but they turn upon the man, who was more *obnoxious* to them, and they tell him that it was not lawful for him to carry his bed that day [*John* v. 10].

Donne, *Sermon* 20.

Examine thyself in the particulars of thy relations; especially where thou governest and takest accounts of others, and art not so *obnoxious* to them as they to thee.

J. Taylor, *The Worthy Communicant*, c. vi. sect. 2.

What shall we then say of the power of God Himself to dispose of men? little, finite, *obnoxious* things of his own making?

South, *Sermons*, 1744, vol. viii. p. 315.

OBSEQUIOUS, OBSEQUIOUSNESS. There lies ever in 'obsequious' at the present the sense of an observance which is overdone, of an unmanly readiness to fall in with the will of another; there lay nothing of this in the Latin 'obsequium,' nor yet in our English word as employed two centuries ago.

Besides many other fishes in divers places, which are very obeisant and *obsequious*, when they be called by their names.

Holland, *Plutarch's Morals*, p. 970.

His corrections are so far from compelling men to come to heaven, as that they put many men farther out of their way, and work an obduration rather than an *obsequiousness*.

Donne, *Sermon* 45.

In her relation to the king she was the best pattern of conjugal love and *obsequiousness*.

Bates, *Sermon upon the Death of the Queen.*

OCCUPY, OCCUPIER. He now 'occupies,' who has in present possession; but the word involved once the further signification of using, employing, laying out that which was thus possessed; and by an 'occupier' was meant a trader or retail dealer.

He [Eumenes] made as though he had occasion to *occupy* money, and so borrowed a great sum of them.

North, *Plutarch's Lives,* p. 505.

If they bind me fast with new ropes that never were *occupied,* then shall I be weak, and be as another man.

Judges xvi. 11. Authorized Version.

Mercury, the master of merchants aud *occupiers* [ἀγοραίων].

Holland, *Plutarch's Morals,* p. 692.

OFFAL. This, bearing its derivation on its front, namely, that it is that which, as refuse and of little or no worth, is suffered or caused to *fall off*, we restrict at the present to the refuse of the butcher's stall; but it was once employed in a much wider acceptation.

Glean not in barren soil these *offal* ears,
Sith reap thou may'st whole harvests of delight.

Southwell, *Lewd Love is Loss.*

Poor Lazarus lies howling at his gates for a few crumbs; he only seeks chippings, *offals;* let him roar and howl, famish and eat his own flesh; he respects him not.

Burton, *The Anatomy of Melancholy,* part iii. sect. 1.

OFFICIOUS, OFFICIOUSNESS. Again and again we light on words used once in a good, but now in an unfavorable, sense. An 'officious' person is now a busy uninvited meddler in matters which do not belong to him; so late as Burke's time he might be one prompt and forward in due *offices* of kindness. The more honorable use of 'officious' now only survives in the distinction familiar to diplomacy between an 'official' and 'officious' communication.

> With granted leave *officious* I return.
>
> Milton, *Paradise Regained*, b. ii.

> *Officious*, ready to do good offices, serviceable, friendly, very courteous and obliging.
>
> Phillips, *The New World of Words*.

> They [the nobility of France] were tolerably well bred, very *officious*, humane, and hospitable.
>
> Burke, *Reflections on the Revolution in France*, p. 251.

> Which familiar and affectionate *officiousness* and sumptuous cost, together with that sinister fame that woman was noted with [*Luke* vii. 37], could not but give much scandal to the Pharisees there present.
>
> H. More, *On Godliness*, b. viii. c. 13.

ORIENT. There was once a beautiful use of 'orient' as clear, bright, shining, which has now wholly departed from it. So entirely was all notion of 'eastern' sometimes dropped from the word, that in Milton's sublime Ode on the Nativity, the *setting* sun is said to "pillow his chin upon an *orient* wave." In like manner 'orient,' as so often applied to the pearl by our earlier poets, does not in this connection mean 'oriental,' but pellucid, white, shining. It is not of course denied that the meaning here claimed for 'orient' accrued to it originally from the greater clearness and lightness of the east, as the quarter whence the day broke.

Those shells that keep in the main sea, and lie deeper than that the sunbeams can pierce unto them, keep the finest and most delicate pearls. And yet they, as *orient* as they be, wax yellow with age.

Holland, *Pliny*, part i. p. 255.

Her wings and train of feathers, mixed fine
Of *orient* azure and incarnadine.

Sylvester, *Du Bartas, Fifth Day.*

Κόκκος βαφική, a shrub, whose red berries or grains gave an *orient* tincture to cloth.

Fuller, *A Pisgah Sight of Palestine*, b. iv. c. 6.

OSTLER. Not formerly, as now, the servant of the inn, having care of the horses, but the innkeeper or host, the 'hosteller' himself.

And another dai he broughte forth tweie pens, and gaf to the *ostler* [stabulario, Vulg.].

Luke x. 35. Wiclif.

The *innkeeper* was old, fourscore almost;
Indeed an emblem, rather than an host;
In whom we read how God and Time decree
To honour thrifty *ostlers*, such as he.

Corbet, *Iter Boreale.*

P.

PAINFUL, PAINFULNESS, PAINFULLY. 'Painful' is now feeling pain, or inflicting it; it was once taking pains. Many things would not be so 'painful' in the present sense of the word, if they had been more 'painful' in the earlier, as perhaps some sermons.

Within fourteen generations, the royal blood of the kings of Judah ran in the veins of plain Joseph, a *painful* carpenter.

Fuller, *The Holy War,* b. v. c. 29.

O the holiness of their living, and *painfulness* of their preaching.

Id., *The Holy State,* b. ii. c. 6.

Whoever would be truly thankful, let him live in some honest vocation, and therein bestow himself faithfully and *painfully.*

Sanderson, *Sermons,* vol. i. p. 251.

PALLIATE, PALLIATION. 'To palliate' is at this day to extenuate a fault through the setting out of whatever will best serve to diminish the estimate of its gravity; and does not imply any endeavor wholly to deny it; nay, implies rather a certain recognition and admission of the fault itself. Truer to its etymology once, it expressed the *cloking* of it, the attempt, successful or otherwise, entirely to conceal and cover it. Eve 'palliates' her fault in the modern sense of the word (*Gen.* iii. 13), Gehazi in the earlier (2 *Kings* v. 25).

You cannot *palliate* mischief, but it will
Through all the fairest coverings of deceit
Be always seen.

Daniel, *The Tragedy of Philotas*, Act iv. Sc. 2.

You see the Devil could fetch up nothing of Samuel at the request of Saul, but a shadow and a resemblance, his countenance and his mantle, which yet was not enough to cover the cheat, or to *palliate* the illusion.

South, *Sermon on Easter Day*.

The generality of Christians make the external frame of religion but a *palliation* for sin.

H. More, *The Grand Mystery of Godliness*, p. ix.

PANTOMIME. Now the mimic show itself, but at the first introduction of the word (Bacon's constant use of 'pantomimus' and 'pantomimi' testifies that it was new in his time), the player who presented the show.

You shall have a buffoon or *pantomimus* shall express as many [voices] as he pleaseth.

Bacon, *The Advancement of Learning*, b. ii.

I would our *pantomimes* also and stage-players would examine themselves and their callings by this rule.

Sanderson, *Sermon on* 1 *Cor.* vii. 24.

Not that I think those *pantomimes*
Who vary action with the times,
Are less ingenious in their art
Than those who dully act one part.

Butler, *Hudibras*, part iii. c. 2.

PATHETIC, PATHETICAL, PATHETICALLY. The 'pathetic' is now only *one* kind of the passionate, that which, feeling *pity*, is itself capable of stirring it;

but 'pathetic' or 'pathetical' and 'passionate' were once of an equal reach. When in a language like ours two words, derived from two different languages, as in this case from the Greek and from the Latin, exist side by side, being at the same time identical in signification, the desynonymizing process which we may note here, continually comes into play.

He [Hiel, cf. 1 *Kings* xvi. 34] mistook Joshua's curse rather for a *pathetical* expression than prophetical prediction.

Fuller, *A Pisgah Sight of Palestine*, b. ii. c. 12.

Whatever word enhanceth Joseph's praise,
Her echo doubles it, and doth supply
Some more *pathetic* and transcendent phrase
To raise his merit.

Beaumont, *Psyche*, c. i. st. 148.

For Truth, I know not how, hath this unhappiness fatal to her, ere she can come to the trial and inspection of the understanding; being to pass through many little wards and limits of the several affections and desires, she cannot shift it, but must put on such colours and attire as those *pathetical* handmaids of the soul please to lead her in to their queen.

Milton, *The Reason of Church Government*, b. ii. c. 3.

But the principal point whereon our apostle pitcheth for evincing the priesthood of Christ to be far more excellent than the Levitical priesthood was, was reserved to the last, and *pathetically* though briefly avouched, ver. 20 [*Heb.* vii. 20].

Jackson, *Of the Divine Essence and Attributes*, b. ix. § 2.

PEEVISH, PEEVISHNESS. By 'peevishness' we now understand a small but constantly fretting ill-temper; yet no one can read our old authors, with whom 'peevish' and 'peevishness' are of constant recurrence, without feeling that their use of them is different from ours; although precisely to determine what their use was is any thing but easy. Gifford (*Massinger*, vol. i. p. 71) says confidently, "peevish is foolish;" but upon induction from an insufficient number of passages. 'Peevish' is rather self-willed, obstinate. That in a world like ours those who refuse to give up their own wills should be continually crossed, and thus should become fretful, and 'peevish' in our modern sense of the word, is inevitable; and here is the history of the change of meaning which it has undergone.

> *Valentine.* Cannot your grace win her to fancy him?
> *Duke.* No, trust me; she is *peevish*, sullen, forward,
> Proud, disobedient, stubborn, lacking duty.
> Shakespeare, *The Two Gentlemen of Verona*, Act iii. Sc. 1.

We provoke, rail, scoff, calumniate, challenge, hate, abuse (hard-hearted, implacable, malicious, *peevish*, inexorable as we are), to satisfy our lust or private spleen.

Burton, *The Anatomy of Melancholy*, part iii. § 1.

Pertinax hominum genus, a *peevish* generation of men.

Id., *Ib.* part iii. § 4.

That grand document of keeping to the light within us they [the Quakers] borrow out of S. John's Gospel; and yet they are so frantic and *peevish*, that they would fling away the staff without which they are not able to make one step in religion.

H. More, *The Grand Mystery of Godliness*, b. viii. c. 12.

In case the Romans, upon an inbred *peevishness* and engraffed pertinacity of theirs, should not hear reason, but refuse an indifferent end, then both God and man shall be witness as well of the moderation of Perseus, as of their pride and insolent frowardness.

Holland, *Livy*, p. 1152.

We must carefully distinguish continuance in opinion from obstinacy, confidence of understanding from *peevishness* of affection, a not being convinced from a resolution never to be convinced.

J. Taylor, *The Liberty of Prophesying*, § ii. 10.

PENCIL. The distinction between 'pencil' and paint-brush, with the employment of 'pencil' in any other sense than that of brush, is quite of modern introduction. The older use of the word, it needs hardly to say, was etymologically more correct than the modern, 'pencil' being 'pencillus,' or little tail; and the brush was so called because it hung and drooped as this does.

Heaven knows, they were besmeared and overstained
With slaughter's *pencil*, where revenge did paint
The fearful difference of incensed kings.

Shakespeare, *King John*, Act iii. Sc. 1.

Learning is necessary to him [the heretic], if he trades in a critical error; but if he only broaches dregs, and deals in some dull sottish opinion, a trowel will serve as well as a *pencil* to daub on such thick coarse colours.

Fuller, *The Profane State*, b. v. c. 10.

The first thing she did after rising was to have recourse to the *red-pot*, out of which she laid it on very thick with a *pencil*, not only on her cheeks, chin, under the nose, above the eyebrows and edges of the ears, but also on the inside of her hands, her fingers, and shoulders.

The Lady's Travels in Spain, Letter 8.

PENITENTIARY. It is curious that this word has possessed three entirely independent meanings, penitent, ordainer of penances in the Church, and place for penitents; only the last survives.

So Manasseh in the beginning and middle of his reign filled the city with innocent blood, and died a *penitentiary*.

Jackson, *Christ's Session at the Right Hand of God,* b. ii. c. 42.

'Twas a French friar's conceit that courtiers were of all men the likeliest to forsake the world and turn *penitentiaries*.

Hammond, *The Seventh Sermon, Works,* vol. iv. p. 517.

Penitentiary, a priest that imposes upon an offender what penance he thinks fit.

Phillips, *The New World of Words.*

Penury. This expresses now no more than the objective fact of extreme poverty ; an ethical subjective meaning not lying in it, as would sometimes of old, but now only retained in 'penurious.'

God sometimes punishes one sin with another; pride with adultery, drunkenness with murder, carelessness with irreligion, idleness with vanity, *penury* with oppression.

J. Taylor, *The Faith and Patience of the Saints.*

Perseverance. It is difficult to connect the uses of 'perseverance' whereof examples are given below, and they might easily be multiplied, with its more frequent use of old, and its sole use at present. Indeed I have sometimes doubts whether it be the same word at all, and whether we are not to look to 'seperare,' 'sevrer,' 'severance' (it might thus be the power of dividing and distinguishing), for its root rather than to 'perseverantia.' None of our Dictionaries give any assistance in the matter; indeed they have not noted this use of the word; but there is a good collection of illustrative passages in *Notes and Queries*, No. 182.

For his diet he [Ariosto] was very temperate, and a great enemy of excess and surfeiting, and so careless of delicates as though he had no *perseverance* for the taste of meats.

Sir J. Harington, *Life of Ariosto*, p. 418.

He [Æmilius Paulus] suddenly fell into a raving (without any *perseverance* of sickness spied in him before, or any change or alteration in him [πρὶν αἰσθέσθαι καὶ νοῆσαι τὴν μεταβολήν]), and his wits went from him in such sort that he died three days after.

North, *Plutarch's Lives*, p. 221.

Person. We have forfeited the full force of the statement, "God is no respecter of *persons*;" from the fact that 'person' does not mean for us now all that it once meant. 'Person,' from 'persona,' the mask constantly worn by the actor of antiquity, is, by natural transfer, the part or *rôle* in the play which each sustains, as πρόσωπον is in Greek. In the great tragi-comedy of life each sustains a 'person;' one that of a king, another that of a hind; one must play Dives, another Lazarus. This 'person' God, for whom the question is not, *what* 'person' each sustains, but *how* he sustains it, does not regard.

King. What, rate, rebuke, and roughly send to prison
The immediate heir of England! was this easy?
May this be washed in Lethe, and forgotten?
Chief Justice. I then did use the *person* of your father;
The image of his power lay then in me.

Shakespeare, 2 *Henry IV*. Act v. Sc. 2.

Cæsar also is brought in by Julian attributing to himself the honour (if it were at all an honour to that *person* which he sustained), of being the first that left his ship and took land.

Milton, *The History of England*, b. ii.

Certain it is, that no man can long put on a *person* and act a part but his evil manners will peep through the corners of his white robe, and God will bring a hypocrite to shame even in the eyes of men.

J. Taylor, *Apples of Sodom.*

PERSPECTIVE. 'Telescope' and 'microscope' are both as old as Milton; but for a long while 'perspective' (glass being sometimes understood, and sometimes expressed) did the work of these. It is sometimes written 'prospective.' Our present use of 'perspective' does not, I suppose, date farther back than Dryden.

While we look for incorruption in the heavens, we find they are but like the earth, durable in their main bodies, alterable in their parts; whereof, beside comets and new stars, *perspectives* begin to tell tales; and the spots that wander about the sun, with Phaeton's favour, would make clear conviction.

Sir T. Browne, *Hydriotaphia.*

Look through faith's *perspective* with the magnifying end on invisibles (for such is its frame, it lesseneth visibles), and thou wilt see sights not more strange than satisfying.

Whitlock, *Zootomia*, p. 535.

A tiny mite which we can scarcely see
Without a *perspective.*

Oldham, *Eighth Satire of M. Boileau.*

PESTER. There is no greater discomfort or annoyance than extreme straightness or narrowness of room;

out of which in Greek στενοχωρία, signifying this, has come to have a secondary signification of trouble or anguish. In English, to 'pester' bears witness to the same fact, though it has travelled in exactly the opposite direction, and having first the meaning of to vex or annoy, which meaning it still retains, had also once a second meaning of painfully cooping-up in a narrow and confined space; which, however, it now has let go.

Now because the most part of the people might not possibly have a sight of him, they gat up all at once into the theatre, and *pestered* it quite full.

Holland, *Livy*, p. 1055.

They within, though *pestered* with their own numbers, stood to it like men resolved, and in a narrow compass did remarkable deeds.

Milton, *The History of England*, b. ii.

The calendar is filled, not to say, *pestered* with them, jostling one another for room, many holding the same day in copartnership of festivity.

Fuller, *The Worthies of England*, c. 3.

PLACARD. Formerly used often in the sense of a license or permission, the 'placard' being properly the broad tablet or board on which this, as well as other edicts and ordinances, was exposed.

Then for my voice I must (no choice)
Away of force, like posting horse,
For sundry men had *placards* then
  Such child to take.

Tusser, *The Author's Life.*

Others are of the contrary opinion, and that Christianity gives us a *placard* to use these sports; and that man's charter of dominion over the creatures enables him to employ them as well for pleasure as necessity.

Fuller, *The Holy State*, b. iii. c. 13.

PLANTATION. We still 'plant' a colony, but a 'plantation' is now of trees only; and not of men, as it was when 'The Plantations' was the standing name by which our transatlantic colonies were known.

It is a shameful and unblessed thing to take the scum of people and wicked condemned men to be the people with whom you plant; and not only so, but it spoileth the *plantation*.

Bacon, *Essays*, 33.

Plantations make mankind broader, as generation makes it thicker.

Fuller, *The Holy State*, b. iii. c. 16.

PLAUSIBLE, PLAUSIBLY, PLAUSIBILITY. That is 'plausible' now which presents itself as worthy of applause; yet always with a subaudition, or at least a suggestion, that it is not so really; it was once that which obtained applause, with at least the *primâ facie* likelihood that the applause which it obtained it deserved.

This John, Bishop of Constantinople, that assumed to himself the title of Universal Bishop or Patriarch, was a good man, given greatly to alms and fasting, but too much addicted to advance the title of his see; which made a *plausible* bishop seem to be Antichrist to Gregory the Great.

Hacket, *The Life of Archbishop Williams*, part ii. p. 66.

The Romans *plausibly* did give consent
For Tarquin's everlasting banishment.

Shakespeare, *The Rape of Lucrece.*

He was no sooner in sight than every one received him *plausibly*, and with great submission and reverence.

Stubs, *The Anatomy of Abuses*, p. 17.

Being placed in the upper part of the world, [he] carried on his dignity with that justice, modesty, integrity, fidelity, and other gracious *plausibilities*, that in a place of trust he contented those whom he could not satisfy, and in a place of envy procured the love of those who emulated his greatness.

Vaughan, *The Life and Death of Dr. Jackson.*

POACH, POACHER. It sounds strange to say that 'poker' and 'poacher' are in fact one and the same word; which, doubtless, they are. A 'poacher' is, strictly speaking, an intruder, the word means nothing more; one who intrudes, 'pokes,' or 'poaches' into land where he has no business; the fact that he does so with the intention of spoiling the game is superadded, not lying in the word.

So that, to speak truly, they [the Spaniards] have rather *poached* and offered at a number of enterprises, than maintained any constantly.

Bacon, *Notes of a Speech concerning a War with Spain*

It is ill conversing with an ensnarer, delving into the bottom of your mind, to know what is hid in it. I would ask a casuist if it were not lawful for me not only to hide my mind, but to cast something that is not true before such a *poacher*.

Hacket, *The Life of Archbishop Williams*, part ii. p. 113.

POLITICS, POLITICIAN. At the present 'politics' are always *things*, but were sometimes *persons* as well in times past. 'Politician' also had mostly an evil subaudition. One so named was a trickster or underhand self-seeker in politics, or it might be, as it is throughout in the sermon of South, quoted below, in the ordinary affairs of life.

It did in particular exasperate Tacitus, and other *politicks* of his temper, to see so many natural Romans renounce their name and country for maintenance of Jewish religion.

Jackson, *The Eternal Truth of Scriptures*, b. i. c. 20.

Why, look you, I am whipped and scourged with rods,
Nettled and stung with pismires, when I hear
Of this vile *politician* Bolingbroke.

Shakespeare, 1 *Henry IV.*, Act i. Sc. 8.

The *politician*, whose very essence lies in this, that he is a person ready to do any thing that he apprehends for his advantage, must first of all be sure to put himself in a state of liberty, as free and large as his principles, and so to provide elbow-room enough for his conscience to lay about it, and have its full play in.

South, *Sermons*, 1744, vol. i. p. 324.

Pomp.
Pompous,
Pompously.

'Pomp' is one of the many words which Milton employs with a strict classical accuracy, so that he is only to be perfectly understood when we keep in mind that a 'pomp' with him is always πομπή, a procession. He is not, however, singular, as he often is, in the stricter and more rigorous use of this word. It is easy to perceive how 'pomp' obtained its wider application. There is no such favorable opportunity for the display of state and magnificence as a procession; this is almost the inevitable form which they take; and thus the word, which was first applied to the most frequent display of these, came afterwards to be transferred to every display.

In respect of 'pompous' and 'pompously' there is something else to note. There is in them always now the subaudition of that which is more in show than in substance, or, at any rate, of a magnificence which, if real, is yet vaingloriously and ostentatiously displayed. But they conveyed, and were intended to convey, no such impression once.

[Antiochus] also provided a great number of bulls with gilt horns, the which he conducted himself with a goodly *pomp* and procession to the very gate of the city [ἄχρι τῶν πυλῶν ἐπόμπευσε].

Holland, *Plutarch's Morals*, p. 417.

With goddess-like demeanour forth she went,
Not unattended; for on her, as queen,
A *pomp* of winning graces waited still.

Milton, *Paradise Lost*, b. viii.

What *pompous* powers of ravishment were here,*
What delicate extremities of pleasure.

Beaumont, *Psyche*, can. xv. st. 299.

All expresses related that the entertainment [of Prince Charles at Madrid] was very *pompous* and kingly.

Hacket, *The Life of Archbishop Williams*, part i. p. 119.

He [Hardecnute] gave his sister Gunildis, a virgin of rare beauty, in marriage to Henry the Alman Emperor; and to send her forth *pompously*, all the nobility contributed their jewels and richest ornaments.

Milton, *The History of England*, b. vi.

POLITE, POLITELY. Between 'polite' and 'polished' this much of difference has now grown up

* In heaven.

and established itself, that 'polite' is always employed in a secondary and tropical sense, having reference to the polish of the mind, while it is free to use 'polished' in the literal and figurative sense alike.

Polite bodies, as looking-glasses.

Cudworth, *The Intellectual System*, p. 731.

Polite; well polished, neat.

Phillips, *The New World of Words.*

In things artificial seldom any elegance is wrought without a superfluous waste and refuse in the transaction. No marble statue can be *politely* carved, no fair edifice built, without almost as much rubbish and sweeping.

Milton, *The Reason of Church Government*, b. i. c. 7.

POPULAR, POPULARITY. } He was 'popular' once, not who had acquired, but who was laying himself out to acquire, the favor of the people. 'Popularity' was the wooing, not as now the having won, that favor. The word which is passive now was active then.

Of a senator he [Manlius] became *popular*, and began to break his mind and impart his designs unto the magistrates of the Commons, finding fault with the nobility.

Holland, *Livy*, p. 224.

And oft in vain his name they closely bite,
As *popular* and flatterer accusing.

P. Fletcher, *The Purple Island*, c. 10.

Cato the Younger charged Muræna, and indited him in open court for *popularity* and ambition.

Holland, *Plutarch's Morals*, p. 243.

Harold, lifted up in mind, and forgetting now his former shows of *popularity*, defrauded his soldiers their due and well-deserved share of the spoils.

Milton, *The History of England*, b. vi.

PORTLY. There lies in 'portly' a certain sense of dignity of demeanor still, but always connoted with this a certain cumbrousness and weight, such as Spenser in his noble *Epithalamion* (see below) would never have ascribed to his bride, as little Shakespeare to the swift-footed Achilles (*Troilus and Cressida*, Act iv. Sc. 5), or to the youthful Romeo.

The chief and most *portly* person of them all was one Hasdrubal [Insignis tamen inter ceteros Hasdrubal erat].

Holland, *Livy*, p. 770.

Lo, where she comes along with *portly* pace,
Like Phœbe from her chamber of the east.

Spenser, *Epithalamion*, 148.

He [Romeo] bears him like a *portly* gentleman.

Shakespeare, *Romeo and Juliet*, Act i. Sc. 5.

PRAGMATICAL. This is always employed at the present in an ill sense; not merely busy, but over-busy, officious, meddling; nay, more than this, with an assumption of bustling self-importance. The etymology of 'pragmatical' does not require this ill sense, which is merely superinduced upon it, and from which it was not indeed always, but often, free in its earlier use.

It may appear at the first a new and unwonted argument, to teach men how to raise and make their fortune; but the handling thereof concerneth learning greatly both in honour and in substance. In honour, because *pragmatical* men may not go away with an opinion that learning is like a lark, that can mount and sing and please herself, and nothing else; but may know that she holdeth as well of the hawk, that can soar aloft, and also descend and strike upon the prey.

Bacon, *The Advancement of Learning*, b. ii.

We cannot always be contemplative or *pragmatical* abroad; but have need of some delightful intermissions, wherein the enlarged soul may leave off her severe schooling.

Milton, *Tetrachordon*.

PREPOSTEROUS, PREPOSTEROUSLY. } A word nearly or quite unserviceable now, being merely an ungraceful and slipshod synonym for absurd. But restore and confine it to its old use and to one peculiar branch of absurdity, the reversing of the true order and method of things, the putting of the last first and the first last, and of what excellent service it would be capable!

It is a *preposterous* order to teach first, and to learn after.

Bible, 1611, *The Translators to the Reader*.

King Asa justly received little benefit by them [physicians], because of his *preposterous* addressing himself to them before he went to God (2 *Chron*. xvi. 12).

Fuller, *The Worthies of England*, c. ix.

Some indeed *preposterously* misplace these, and make us partake of the benefit of Christ's priestly office in the forgiveness of our sins and our reconcilement to God, before we are brought under the sceptre of his kingly office by our obedience.

South, *Sermons*, 1744, vol. ix. p. 3.

PRETEND, PRETENCE, PRETENSION. } To charge one with 'pretending' any thing is now a much more serious charge than it was once. Indeed, it was not necessarily, and only by accident, a charge at all. That was 'pretended' which one stretched out before himself and in face of others; but whether it was the thing it affirmed itself to be, or, as at present, only a deceitful resemblance of this, the word did not decide. While it was thus with 'to pretend,' there was as yet no distinction recognized between 'pretence' and 'pretension;' they both signified the act of 'pretending,' or the thing 'pretended;' but whether truly or falsely it was left to the context, or to the judgment of the reader, to decide. 'Pretence' has since followed the fortunes of 'pretend,' and has fallen with it; while 'pretension' has disengaged itself from being a merely useless synonym of 'pretence,' and, retaining its relations to the earlier uses of the verb, now signifies a claim put forward which may be valid, or may be invalid, the word leaving this for other considerations to determine. Louis Napoleon assumed the dictatorship under the 'pretence, of resisting anarchy; the House of Orleans has 'pretensions' to the throne of France. But these distinctions are quite modern.

Being preferred by King James to the bishopric of Chichester, and *pretending* his own imperfectness and insufficiency to undergo such a charge, he caused to be engraven about the seal of his bishopric, those words of St. Paul, Et ad hæc quis idoneus?

Henry Isaacson, *The Life and Death of Lancelot Andrews.*

[The Sabbath] is rather hominis gratiâ quam Dei; and though God's honour is mainly *pretended* in it, yet it is man's happiness that is really intended by it, even of God Himself.

H. More, *The Grand Mystery of Godliness,* b. viii. c. 13.

Or crafty malice might *pretend* this praise,
And think to ruin, where it seemed to praise.
B. Jonson, *To the Memory of Shakespeare.*

This is the tree whose leaves were intended for the healing of the nations, not for a *pretence* and palliation for sin.
H. More, *The Grand Mystery of Godliness*, b. viii. c. 1.

It is either secret pride, or base faintness of heart, or dull sloth, or some other thing, and not true modesty in us, if, being excellently gifted for some weighty employment in every other man's judgment, we yet withdraw ourselves from it with *pretensions* of unsufficiency.
Sanderson, *Sermons*, 1671, p. 208.

PREVARICATE, PREVARICATION. } This verb, often now very loosely used, had once a very definite meaning of its own. 'To prevaricate' is to betray the cause which one affects to sustain, and, so far as I know, is always so used by our early writers. We have inherited the word from the Latin law-courts, which borrowed it from the life. The 'prævaricator' being one who halted on two unequal legs, the name was transferred to him who, affecting to prosecute a charge, was in secret collusion with the opposite party, and so managed the cause as to ensure his escape. Observe in the two following passages the accuracy of use which so habitually distinguishes our writers of the seventeenth century as compared with too many of the nineteenth.

I proceed now to do the same service for the divines of England; whom you question first in point of learning and sufficiency, and then in point of conscience and honesty, as *prevaricating* in the religion which they possess, and inclining to Popery.
Chillingworth, *The Religion of Protestants*, Preface, p. 11.

If we be not all enemies to God in this kind [in a direct opposition]; yet in adhering to the enemy we are enemies; in our *prevarications*, and easy betrayings and surrendering of ourselves to the enemy of his kingdom, Satan, we are his enemies.

Donne, *Sermon 7, On the Nativity.*

PREVENT. One may reach a point before another to help or to hinder him there; may anticipate his arrival either with the purpose of keeping it *for* him, or keeping it *against* him. 'To prevent' has slipped by very gradual degrees, which it would not be difficult to trace, from the sense of keeping *for* to that of keeping *against*, from the sense of arriving first with the intention of helping, to that of arriving first with the intention of hindering, and then generally from helping to hindering.

So it is, that if Titus had not *prevented* the whole multitude of people which came to see him, and if he had not got him away betimes, before the games were ended, he had hardly escaped from being stifled amongst them.

North, *Plutarch's Lives*, p. 321.

Gentlemen that were brought low, not by their vices, but by misfortune, *poveri vergognosi* as the Tuscan calls them, bashful, and could not crave though they perished, he *prevented* their modesty, and would heartily thank those that discovered their commiserable condition to him.

Hacket, *The Life of Archbishop Williams*, part i. p. 201.

There he beheld how humbly diligent
New Adulation was to be at hand;
How ready Falsehood stept; how nimbly went
Base pick-thank Flattery, and *prevents* command.

Daniel, *Civil Wars*, b. ii. st. 56.

PRODIGIOUS. This notes little now but magnitude. Truer to its etymology once ('prodigium' = 'pro-dicium,' and that from 'prodico'), it signified the ominous, or ominously prophetic.

Blood shall put out your torches, and instead
Of gaudy flowers about your wanton necks,
An axe shall hang, like a *prodigious* meteor,
Ready to crop your loves' sweets.

Beaumont and Fletcher, *Philaster*, Act v. Sc. 1.

Without this comely ornament of hair, their [women's] most glorious beauty appears as deformed, as the sun would be *prodigious* without beams.

Fuller, *The Profane State*, b. v. c. 5.

I began to reflect on the whole life of this *prodigious* man.

Cowley, *On the Government of Oliver Cromwell.*

PROMOTE, PROMOTER, PROMOTION. 'To promote,' that is, to further or set forward, a 'promoter,' a furtherer, are now words of harmless, often of quite an honorable, signification. They were once terms of extremest scorn; a 'promoter' being a common informer, and so called because he 'promoted' charges and accusations against men (promotor litium: Skinner).

Thou Linus, that lov'st still to be *promoting*,
Because I sport about King Henry's marriage,
Think'st this will prove a matter worth the carriage.

Sir J. Harington, *Epigrams*, ii. 98.

Aristogiton the sycophant, or false *promotor*, was condemned to death for troubling men with wrongful imputations.

Holland, *Plutarch's Morals*, p. 421.

His eyes be *promoters*, some trespass to spy.
Tusser, *Description of an envious and haughty Neighbour.*

Promoters be those which in popular and penal actions do defer the names or complain of offenders, having part of the profit for their reward.
Cowell, *The Interpreter*, 1637.

Covetousness and *promotion* and such like are that right hand and right eye which must be cut off and plucked out, that the whole man perish not.
Tyndale, *Exposition of the Sixth Chap. of Matthew.*

Propriety. All 'propriety' is now mental or moral; where material things are concerned, 'property' is the word which we use. It needs hardly to say that 'propriety' and 'property' were at the first no more than different spellings or slightly different forms of one and the same word; which now, however, have been thus usefully desynonymized.

He provides good bounds and sufficient fences betwixt his own and his master's estate (Jacob, *Gen.* xxx. 36, set his flock three days' journey from Laban's), that no quarrel may arise about their *propriety*, nor suspicion that his remnant hath eaten up his master's whole cloth.
Fuller, *The Holy State*, b. i. c. 8.

Hail, wedded love, mysterious law, true source
Of human offspring, sole *propriety*
In Paradise of all things common else.
Milton, *Paradise Lost*, b. v.

Prose, Proser. 'To prose' is now to talk or to write heavily, tediously, without spirit and without animation; but 'to prose was once the antithesis of to versify, and a 'proser' of a writer in metre.

In the tacit assumption that vigor, animation, rapid movement, with all the precipitation of the spirit, belong to verse rather than to prose, lies the explanation of the changed uses of the words.

It was found that whether ought was imposed me by them that had the overlooking, or betaken to of mine own choice in English or other tongue, *prosing* or versing, but chiefly this latter, the style, by certain vital signs it had, was likely to live.

Milton, *The Reason of Church Government*, b. ii.

And surely Nash, though he a *proser* were,
A branch of laurel yet deserves to bear.

Drayton, *On Poets and Poesy.*

PRUNE. At present we only 'prune' trees; but our earlier authors use the word where we should use 'preen,' which indeed is but another form of the word; nay, with a wider signification; for with us only birds 'preen' their feathers, while women, as in the example which follows, might 'prune' themselves of old.

A husband that loveth to trim and pamper his body, causeth his wife by that means to study nothing else but the tricking and *pruning* of herself.

Holland, *Plutarch's Morals*, p. 318.

PUNCTUAL, PUNCTUALLY. } Restricted now to the accurate observing of fixed *points* of *time*. It had once a wider use; a 'punctual' narration being a narration which entered into minuter *points* of detail.

Truly I thought I could not be too *punctual* in describing the animal life, it being so serviceable for our better understanding the divine.

H. More, *The Grand Mystery of Godliness*, Preface, p. x.

All curious solicitude about riches smells of avarice; even the very disposing of it with a too *punctual* and artificial liberality is not worth a painful solicitude.

Cotton, *Montaigne's Essays*, b. iii. c. 9.

Every one is to give a reason of his faith; but priests or ministers more *punctually* than any.

H. More, *The Grand Mystery of Godliness*, b. x. c. 12.

PUNY. The present use of 'puny,' as that which is at once weak and small, is only secondary and inferential. 'Puny' or 'puisne' (puis né) is born after another, therefore younger; and only by inference smaller and weaker.

It were a sign of ignorant arrogancy, if *punies* or freshmen should reject the axioms and principles of Aristotle, usual in the schools, because they have some reasons against them which themselves cannot answer.

Jackson, *The Eternal Truth of Scriptures*, c. i.

[The worthy soldier] had rather others should make a ladder of his dead corpse to scale a city by it, than a bridge of him whilst alive for his *punies* to give him the go-by, and pass over him to preferment.

Fuller, *The Holy State*, b. iv. c. 17.

He is dead and buried, and by this time no *puny* among the mighty nations of the dead; for though he left this world not very many days past, yet every hour, you know, addeth largely unto that dark society.

Sir T. Browne, *Letter to a Friend*, p. 1.

PURSUER. 'Pursue' and 'pursuer' are older words in the language than 'persecute' and 'persecutor'—earlier adoptions of 'persequor' and 'persecutor,' and not, as these last, immediately from the Latin. Beside the meaning which they still retain, they once also covered the meanings which these later words have, since their introduction, appropriated as exclusively their own.

I first was a blasphemer and *pursuwer*.

1 *Tim.* i. 13. Wiclif.

If God leave them in this hardness of heart, they may prove as desperate opposites and *pursuers* of all grace, of Christ and Christians, as the most horrible open swine, as we see in Saul and Julian.

Rogers, *Naaman the Syrian*, p. 106.

Q.

QUAINT, QUAINTLY. In 'quaint,' which is the Latin 'comptus,' there lies always now the notion of a certain curiosity and oddness, however these may be subordinated to ends of beauty and grace, and indeed may themselves be made to contribute to these ends; but all this is of late introduction into the word, which had once simply the meaning of elegant, graceful, skilful, subtle.

O brotel joye, O swete poison *queinte*,
O monstre that so sotilly canst peinte
Thy giftes, under hewe of stedfastness,
That thou deceivest bothe more and less.

Chaucer, *The Merchantes Tale.*

But you, my lord, were glad to be employed
To show how *quaint* an orator you are.

Shakespeare, 2 *Henry VI.*, Act iii. Sc. 2.

Whom evere I schal kisse, he it is; holde ye him, and lede ye warli, *or queyntly*.

Mark xiv. 44. Wiclif.

A ladder *quaintly* made of cords.

Shakespeare, *The Two Gentlemen of Verona*, Act iii. Sc. 1.

QUERULOUS. Not once, as now, complaining, but quarrelsome. As there is no 'querulosus' in Latin, I am inclined to think that 'quarrellous' was the earlier form, though I do not remember to have met it.

There inhabit these regions a kind of people, rude, warlike, ready to fight, *querulous*, and mischievous.

Holland, *Camden's Scotland*, p. 39.

R.

RACE. 'Racy' still exists as an epithet applied to that which, growing out of a strong and vigorous *root*, tastes of that root out of which it grows; but 'race,' in the sense of root imparting these qualities, is not any longer in use.

I think the Epistles of Phalaris to have more *race*, more spirit, more force of wit and genius, than any other I have ever seen, either ancient or modern.

Sir William Temple, *Works*, vol. iii. p. 463.

RAISIN. It is conveniently agreed now that 'raisin' shall be employed only of the *dried* grape, but this does not lie in 'racemus,' from which it is descended, nor yet in its earlier uses; indeed, "raisins *of the sun*" (Sir J. Harington) was the phrase commonly employed when our dried fruit was intended.

Nether in the vyneyerd thou schalt gadere *reysyns* and greynes fallynge doun, but thou schalt leeve to be gaderid of pore men and pilgryms.

Lev. xix. 10. Wiclif.

RATHER. This survives for us now only as an adverb, that part of speech to which so many others seem to tend; but meets us often in old English in its prior form, that is, as an adjective; being properly the comparative of 'rathe,' a synonym for early.

This is he that I seide of, aftir me is comen a man, whiche was made bifor me, for he was *rather* than I [quia *prior* me erat, Vulg.].

John i. 30. Wiclif.

If the world hatith you, wite ye that it hadde me in hate *rather* than you [me *priorem* vobis odio habuit, Vulg.].

John xv. 18. Wiclif.

Whatsoever thou or such other say, I say that the pilgrimage that now is used is to them that do it, a praiseable and a good mean to come the *rather* to grace.

Foxe, *Book of Martyrs; Examination of William Thorpe.*

The *rather* lambs been starved with cold.

Spenser, *The Shepherd's Calendar, February.*

RECOGNIZE. This verb means now to revive our knowledge of a person or thing—and nothing more. But in earlier usage there was something further imported into it. It was to revive this knowledge with a purpose—as in the passage below, with the purpose of revision.

In *recognizing* this history I have employed a little more labour, partly to enlarge the argument which I took in hand, partly also to assay, whether by any painstaking I might pacify the stomachs, or to satisfy the judgments of these importune quarrellers.

Foxe, *The Book of Martyrs; Epistle Dedicatory* [*of the Second Edition*] *to the Queen's Majesty.*

REDUCE. That which is 'reduced' now is brought back to narrower limits, or lower terms, or more subject conditions, than those under which it subsisted before. But nothing of this lies of necessity in the word, nor yet in the earlier uses of it. According to these that was 'reduced' which was brought back to its former estate, an estate that might be, and in all the following examples is, an ampler, larger, or more prosperous one than that which it superseded.

The drift of the Roman armies and forces was not to bring free states into servitude, but contrariwise, to *reduce* those that were in bondage to liberty.

Holland, *Livy*, p. 1211.

There remained only Britain [*i. e.* Brittany] to be reunited, and so the monarchy of France to be *reduced* to the ancient terms and bounds.

Bacon, *The History of King Henry VII.*

That He might have these keys to open the heavenly Hades to *reduced* apostates, to penitent, believing, self-devoting sinners, for this it was necessary He should put on man, become obedient to death, even that servile punishment, the death of the cross.

Howe, *The Redeemer's Dominion over the Invisible World.*

RELIGION. Not, as too often now, used as equivalent for godliness; but like θρησκεία, for which it stands *Jam.* i. 27, it expressed the outer form and embodiment which the inward spirit of a true or a false devotion assumed.

We would admit and grant them, that images used for no *religion*, or superstition rather, we mean of none worshipped, nor in danger to be worshipped of any, may be suffered.

Homilies; Sermon against Peril of Idolatry.

By falsities and lies the greatest part
Of mankind they corrupted to forsake
God their Creator, and the invisible
Glory of Him that made them to transform
Oft to the image of a brute, adorned
With gay *religions* full of pomp and gold.

Milton, *Paradise Lost*, b. i.

REMONSTRATE, REMONSTRANCE. Its present sense, namely, to expostulate, was only at a very late date superinduced on the word. 'To remonstrate' is properly to make *any* representation in regard to some step that has been taken. It is now only such show or representation *as protests against* this step; and always assumes this step to have been distasteful: but this limitation lies not of necessity in the word; nor did it lie in its earlier uses.

Properties of a faithful servant: a sedulous eye, to observe all occasions within or without, tending to *remonstrate* the habit within.

Rogers, *Naaman the Syrian*, p. 309.

When Sir Francis Cottington returned with our king's oath, plighted to the annexed conditions for the ease of the Roman Catholics, the Spaniards made no *remonstrance* of joy, or of an ordinary liking to it.

Hacket, *The Life of Archbishop Williams*, part i. p. 145.

Remorse. In the single phrase "without remorse," as in 'remorseless,' we still retain a sense of 'remorse' which otherwise has quite passed away from it; employing it as equivalent with pity. It was thus, as I am inclined to think, that the word acquired this meaning. There is nothing which is followed in natures not absolutely devilish with so swift revulsion of mind as acts of cruelty. No where does the conscience so quickly *remord*, if one may use the word, the guilty actor as in and after these;* and thus 'remorse,' which is the penitence of the natural man,

* A passage of wonderful beauty in one of the Scotch ballads exemplifies what is said above. The Gordon has surrounded and set fire to the castle of an enemy. The daughter, as a last hope of escape, is let down from the wall:—

They rowd her in a pair of sheets,
And towd her owre the wa';
But on the point of Gordon's spear
She gat a deadly fa'.

Then wi' his spear he turned her owre,
O, gin her face was wan!
He said, "Ye are the first that eir
I wished alive again."

He turned her owre and owre again,
Oh, gin her face was white!
"I might ha' spared that bonnie face
To hae bin some man's delight!"

the penitence not wrought by the spirit of grace, while it means the revulsion of the mind and conscience against any evil which has been done, came to mean predominantly revulsion against acts of cruelty, the pity which followed close on these; and thus pity in general, and not only as in this way called out.

King Richard by his own experience grew sensible of the miseries which merchants and mariners at sea underwent. Wherefore, now touched with *remorse* of their pitiful case, he resolved to revoke the law of wrecks.

Fuller, *The Holy War*, b. iii. c. 7.

His helmet, justice, judgment, and *remorse*.

Middleton, *The Wisdom of Solomon*, c. v. 17.

Resent, Resentment. When first introduced into the language (this was in the seventeenth century; 'vox nova in nostrâ linguâ;' Junius), 'to resent' meant to have a sense or feeling of that which had been done to us, but whether a sense of gratitude for the good, or of enmity for the evil, the word itself said nothing, and was employed in both meanings. Must we gather from the fact that the latter is now the exclusive employment of it, that our sense of injuries is much stronger and more lasting than our sense of benefits?

'Tis by my touch alone that you *resent*
What objects yield delight, what discontent.

Beaumont, *Psyche*, can. iv. st. 156.

Perchance as vultures are said to smell the earthliness of a dying corpse; so this bird of prey [the evil Spirit which personated Samuel] *resented* a worse than earthly savour in the soul of Saul, an evidence of his death at hand.

Fuller, *The Profane State*, b. v. c. 4.

The judicious palate will prefer a drop of the sincere milk of the word before vessels full of traditionary pottage, *resenting* of the wild gourd of human invention.

Id., *A Pisgah Sight of Palestine*, b. iii. c. 1.

Sadness does in some cases become a Christian, as being an index of a pious mind, of compassion, and a wise, proper *resentment* of things.

J. Taylor, *Sermon* 23, part ii.

The Council taking notice of the many good services performed by Mr. John Milton, their Secretary for foreign languages, particularly for his book in vindication of the Parliament and people of England against the calumnies and invectives of Salmasius, have thought fit to declare their *resentment* and good acceptance of the same, and that the thanks of the Council be returned to Mr. Milton.

Extract from "The Council-Book," 1651, June 18.

RESTIVE, RESTIVENESS. Any one now invited to define a 'restive' horse would certainly put into his definition that it was one with too much motion; but in obedience to its etymology 'restive' would have once meant one with too little; determined to continue at *rest* when it ought to go forward. Immobile, lazy, stubborn, are the three stages of meaning which the word went through, before it reached its fourth and present.

Bishops or presbyters we know, and deacons we know, but what are chaplains? In state perhaps they may be listed among the upper serving-men of some great man's household, the yeomen ushers of devotion, where the master is too *resty* or too rich to say his own prayers, or to bless his own table.

Milton, *Iconoclastes*, c. xxiv.

Restive, or *Resty*, drawing back instead of going forward, as some horses do.

Phillips, *The New World of Words.*

Nothing hindereth men's fortunes so much as this: Idem manebat, neque idem decebat; men are where they were, when occasions turn. . . . From whatsoever root or cause this *restiveness* of mind proceedeth, it is a thing most prejudicial.

Bacon, *The Advancement of Learning*, b. ii.

The snake, by *restiness* and lying still all winter, hath a certain membrane or film growing over the whole body.

Holland, *Pliny*, part i. p. 210.

RETALIATE, RETALIATION. It has fared with 'retaliate' and 'retaliation' as it has with 'resent' and 'resentment,' that whereas men could once speak of the 'retaliation' of benefits as well as of wrongs, they only 'retaliate' injuries now.

Our captain would not salute the city, except they would *retaliate.*

Diary of Henry Teonge, Aug. 1, 1675.

[The king] expects a return in specie from them [the Dissenters], that the kindness which he has graciously shown them may be *retaliated* on those of his own persuasion.

Dryden, *Preface to The Hind and the Panther.*

His majesty caused directions to be sent for the enlargement of the Roman priests, in *retaliation* for the prisoners that were set at liberty in Spain to congratulate the prince's welcome.

Hacket, *The Life of Archbishop Williams*, part i. p. 166.

RIG. A somewhat vulgar word, with the present use of which, however, we are probably all familiar from its occurrence in *John Gilpin*:—

"He little guessed when he set out
Of running such a *rig*."

But a 'rig' in its earlier use was not so often a strange uncomely *feat*, as a wanton uncomely *person*.

Let none condemn them [the girls] for *rigs* because thus hoyting with the boys, seeing the simplicity of their age was a patent to privilege any innocent pastime.

Fuller, *A Pisgah Sight of Palestine*, b. iv. c. 6.

ROOM. In certain connections we still employ 'room' for place, but in many more, having this meaning once, it has it no longer. Thus the reader who accepts the words of our Authorized Version, "When thou art bidden of any man to a wedding, sit not down in the highest *room*" (*Luke* xiv. 8), according to the present use of 'room' may easily fall into a slight misunderstanding, and imagine to himself guests assembling in various apartments, some more honorable than other; and not, as indeed the meaning is, taking higher or lower *places* at one and the same table.

Is Clarence, Henry, and his son, young Edward,
And all the unlooked-for issue of their bodies,
To take their *rooms*, ere I can place myself?

Shakespeare, 3 *Henry VI.*, Act iii. Sc. 2.

If he have but twelve pence in's purse, he will give it for the best *room* in a playhouse.

Sir T. Overbury, *Characters: A Proud Man.*

RUFFIAN, RUFFIANLY. The Italian 'ruffiano,' the Spanish 'rufian,' the French 'ruffien,' all signify the setter-forward of an infamous traffic between the sexes; nor will the passages quoted below leave any doubt that this is the proper meaning of 'ruffian' in English, others being secondary and derived from it. At the same time the 'ruffian' is not merely the 'leno,' he is the 'amasius' as well; and the frequent allusions to long and elaborately curled hair which go along with the word make one suspect a connection with the Spanish 'rufo,' not as it means red, but crisp or curled. On the possible derivations see Diez, *Roman. Spr.* p. 299.

Our English *ruffians* are metamorphosed into women in their deformed grizzled locks and hair.

Prynne, *Histriomastix*, b. i.

A bawd's furniture, the first a stout *ruffian* to guard her.

Holland's Leaguer, 1632, no pagination.

He [her husband] is no sooner abroad than she is instantly at home, revelling with her *ruffians*.

Reynolds, *God's Revenge against Murder*, b. iii. hist. 11.

Who in London hath not heard of his [Greene's] dissolute and licentious living; his fond disguising of a Master of Art with *ruffianly* hair, unseemly apparel, and more unseemly company?

G. Harvey, *Four Letters touching Robert Greene*, p. 7.

Some frenchified or outlandish monsieur, who hath nothing else to make him famous, I should say infamous, but an effeminate, *ruffianly*, ugly, and deformed lock.

Prynne, *The Unloveliness of Love-Locks*, p. 27.

Rummage. This means at present in the looking for one thing to overturn and unsettle a great many others. It is a sea-term, and signified at first to dispose with such orderly method goods in the hold of a ship that there should be the greatest possible room, or 'roomage.' The quotation from Phillips shows the word in the act of transition from its former use to its present.

And that the masters of the ships do look well to the *romaging*, for they might bring away a great deal more than they do, if they would take pain in the *romaging*.

Hackluyt, *Voyages*, vol. i. p. 308.

To *rummage* (sea-term): To remove any goods or luggage from one place to another, especially to clear the ship's hold of any goods or lading, in order to their being handsomely stowed and placed; whence the word is used upon other occasions, for to rake into, or to search narrowly.

Phillips, *The New World of Words.*

S.

SAD, SADLY, SADNESS. This had once the meaning of earnest, serious, sedate, 'set,' this last being only another form of the same word. The passage from Shakespeare quoted below marks 'sadly' and 'sadness' in their transitional state from the old meaning to the new; Benvolio using 'sadness' in the old sense, Romeo pretending to understand him in the new.

O dere wif, o gemme of lustyhede,
That were to me so *sade*, and eke so trewe.

Chaucer, *The Manciples Tale.*

He may have one year, or two at the most, an ancient and *sad* matron attending on him.

Sir T. Elyot, *The Governor*, b. i. c. 6.

For when I think how far this earth doth us divide,
Alas, meseems, love throws me down; I feel how that I slide.
But then I think again, Why should I thus mistrust
So sweet a wight, so *sad* and wise, that is so true and just?

Surrey, *The Faithful Lover.*

In go the speres *sadly* in the rest.

Chaucer, *The Knightes Tale.*

Therefor ye, britheren, bifor witynge kepe you silf, lest ye be disseyved bi errour of unwise men, and falle awei fro youre owne *sadness* [a propriâ firmitate Vulg.].

2 *Pet.* iii. 17. Wiclif.

Ben. Tell me in *sadness* who she is you love?
Rom. What, shall I groan, and tell you?
Ben. Groan? why, no;
But *sadly* tell me who?

Shakespeare, *Romeo and Juliet,* Act i. Sc. 1.

SASH. At present always a belt or girdle of the loins; not so, however, when first introduced from the East. By the 'sash,' or 'shash' as it was then always spelt, was understood the roll of silk, fine linen, or gauze, worn about the head; in fact a turban.

Shash: Cidaris seu tiara, pileus, Turcicus, ut Doct. Th. H. placet, ab It. Sessa, gausapina cujus involucris Turcæ pileos suos adornant.

Skinner, *Etymologicon.*

So much for the silk in Judea, called Shesh in Hebrew, whence haply that fine linen or silk is called *shashes,* worn at this day about the heads of eastern people.

Fuller, *A Pisgah Sight of Palestine,* b. ii. c. 14.

He [a Persian merchant] was apparelled in a long robe of cloth of gold, his head was wreathed with a huge *shash* or tulipant of silk and gold.

Thomas Herbert, *Travels into divers parts of Asia and Afrique*, 1638, p. 191.

SECURE, SECURITY. In our present English the difference between 'safe' and 'secure' is hardly recognized, but once it was otherwise. 'Secure' ('securus' = sine curâ) was *subjective;* it was a man's own sense, well grounded or not, of the absence of danger; safe was *objective*, the actual fact of such absence of danger. A man, therefore, might *not* be 'safe,' just because he was 'secure' (thus see *Judges* xviii. 7, 10, 27, Authorized Version). I may observe that our use of 'secure' at *Matt.* xxviii. 14, is in fact this early, though we may easily read the passage as though it were employed in the modern sense. "We will *secure* you," of our Version represents ἀμερίμνους ὑμᾶς ποιήσομεν of the original.

We cannot endure to be disturbed or awakened from our pleasing lethargy. For we care not to be safe, but to be *secure*.

J. Taylor, *Of Slander and Flattery*.

They [wicked men] are not *secure*, even when they are safe.

Id., *Apples of Sodom*.

He means, my lord, that we are too remiss,
While Bolingbroke, through our *security*,
Grows strong and great in substance and in friends.

Shakespeare, *King Richard II.*, Act iii. Sc. 2.

The last daughter of pride is delicacy, under which is contained gluttony, luxury, sloth, and *security*.

Nash, *Christ's Tears over Jerusalem*, p. 137.

SEE. Not always confined as now to the *seat* or residence of a bishop; nor indeed did it necessarily involve the notion of a seat *of authority* at all.

> At Babiloine was his soveraine *see*.
>
> Chaucer, *The Monkes Tale.*

> And small harpers with hir glees
> Sate under hem in divers *sees*.
>
> Id., *The House of Fame*, b. iii.

> The Lord smoot all the fyrst gotun in the loond of Egipte, fro the fyrst gotun of Pharao, that sat in his *see*, unto the fyrst gotun of the caitiff woman that was in prisoun.
>
> *Exod.* xii. 29. Wiclif.

SENSUAL, SENSUALITY. 'Sensual' is employed now only in an ill meaning, and implies ever a predominance of sense in provinces where it ought not so to predominate. Milton, feeling that we wanted another word affirming this predominance where no such fault was implied by it, and that 'sensual' only imperfectly expressed this, employed, I know not whether he coined, 'sensuous,' a word which, if it had rooted itself in the language, might have proved of excellent service. 'Sensuality' has had always an ill meaning, but at the same time it was not once the ill meaning which it has now. Any walking by sense and sight rather than by faith was 'sensuality' of old.

> Hath not the Lord Jesus convinced thy *sensual* heart by *sensual* arguments? If thy *sense* were not left-handed, thou mightest with thy right hand bear down thine infidelity; for God hath given assurance sufficient by his Son to thy very *sense*, if thou wert not brutish (1 *John* i. 1).
>
> Rogers, *Naaman the Syrian*, p. 493.

He who might claim this absolute power over the soul to be believed upon his bare word, yet seeing the *sensuality* of man and our woful distrust, is willing to allow us all the means of strengthening our souls in his promise, by such seals and witnesses as confirm it.

Id., *Ib.* p. 483.

A great number of people in divers parts of this realm, following their own *sensuality*, and living without knowledge and due fear of God, do wilfully and schismatically abstain and refuse to come to their own parish churches.

Act of Uniformity, 1661.

SERVILITY. The *subjective* abjectness and baseness of spirit of one who is a slave, or who acts as one, is always implied by this word at the present; while once it did but express the *objective* fact of an outwardly servile condition in him to whom it was ascribed, leaving it possible that in spirit he might be free notwithstanding.

Such *servility* as the Jews endured under the Greeks and Asiatics, have they endured under the Saracen and the Turk.

Jackson, *The Eternal Truth of Scripture*, b. i. c. 26.

The same [faith] inclined Moses to exchange the dignities and delights of a court for a state of vagrancy and *servility*.

Barrow, *Sermon* 3, *On the Apostles' Creed.*

SHEER. It is curious that Christopher Sly's declaration that he was "fourteen pence on the score for *sheer* ale" (*Taming of the Shrew*, *Induction*, Sc. 2) should have given so much trouble to some of our early commentators. 'Sheer,' which is pure, unmixed, was used of things concrete once, but more of things abstract now.

They had scarcely sunk through the uppermost course of sand above, when they might see small sources to boil up, at the first troubled, but afterward they began to yield *sheer* and clear water in great abundance.

Holland, *Livy*, p. 1191.

Thou *sheer*, immaculate, and silver fountain,
From whence this stream through muddy passages
Hath held his current.

Shakespeare, *King Richard II.*, Act v. Sc. 3.

Thou never hadst in thy house, to stay men's stomachs,
A piece of Suffolk cheese, or gammen of bacon,
Or any esculent, but *sheer* drink only,
For which gross fault I here do damn thy license.

Massinger, *A New Way to pay Old Debts*, Act iv. Sc. 2.

SHELF. 'To shelve' as = to shoal, still remains; but not so 'shelf' as = shallow or sand-bank.

I thought fit to follow the rule of coasting maps, where the *shelves* and rocks are described as well as the safe channel.

Davenant, *Preface to Gondibert.*

The watchful hero felt the knocks, and found
The tossing vessel sailed on shoaly ground.
Sure of his pilot's loss, he takes himself
The helm, and steers aloof, and shuns the *shelf.*

Dryden, *Virgil's Æneid*, b. v.

SHREW. There are at the present no 'shrews' save female ones; but the word, like so many others which we have met with, now restrained to one sex, was formerly applied to both. It conveyed also of old a much deeper moral reprobation than now or than in the middle English it did Thus Lucifer is a 'shrew' in *Piers Ploughman*, and two murderers are 'shrews' in the quotation from Chaucer which follows.

And thus accorded ben this *shrewes* tweye
To slea the thridde, as ye han herd me seye.

Chaucer, *The Pardoneres Tale.*

If I schal schewe me innocent, He schal preve me a *schrewe* [*pravum* me comprobabit, Vulg.].

Job ix. 20. Wiclif.

I know none more covetous *shrews* than ye are, when ye have a benefice.

Foxe, *The Book of Martyrs; Examination of William Thorpe.*

SHREWD, SHREWDNESS. } The weakness of the world's moral indignation against evil, causes a multitude of words which once conveyed intensest moral reprobation gradually to convey none at all, or it may be even praise. 'Shrewd' and 'shrewdness' must be numbered among these.

Is he *shrewd* and unjust in his dealings with others?

South, *Sermons*, 1737, vol. vi. p. 106.

Forsothe the erthe is corrupt before God, and is fulfilled with *schrewdnes* [iniquitate, Vulg.].

Gen. vi. 12. Wiclif.

The prophete saith: Flee *shrewdnesse* [declinet a malo, Vulg.], and do goodnesse; seek pees, and folwe it.

Chaucer, *The Tale of Melibeus.*

SIEGE. We employ 'siege' now only of the *sitting down* of an army before a fortified place with the purpose of taking it; but it had once the double meaning, abstract and concrete, of the French 'siége,' a seat.

Whanne mannes sone schal come in his majeste and alle hise aungelis with hym, thanne he schal sitte on the *sege* of his majeste, and alle folkis schal be gaderide bifore hym.

Matt. xxv. 31, 32. Wiclif.

A stately *siege* of soveraine majesty,
And thereon sat a woman gorgeous gay.

Spenser, *The Fairy Queen,* ii. 7, 44.

Besides, upon the very *siege* of justice
Lord Angelo hath to the common ear
Professed the contrary.

Shakespeare, *Measure for Measure,* Act iv. Sc. 2.

SILLY. A deep conviction of men that he who departs from evil will make himself a prey, that none will be a match for the world's evil who is not himself evil, has brought to pass the fact that a number of words, signifying at first goodness, signify next well-meaning simplicity, the notions of goodness and foolishness, with a strong predominance of the last, for a while interpenetrating one another in them, till at length the latter quite expels the former, and remains as the sole possessor of the word. I need hardly mention the Greek εὐήθης, εὐήθεια: while the same has happened in regard of our own 'silly,' which (the same word as the German 'selig,') has successively meant, (1) blessed, (2) innocent, (3) harmless, (4) weakly foolish.

Holofernes, a valiant and mighty captain, being overwhelmed with wine, had his head stricken from his shoulders by that *silly* woman Judith.

Homilies; Sermon against Gluttony and Drunkenness.

This Miles Forest and John Dighton about midnight (the *silly* children lying in their beds) came into the chamber, and suddenly lapped them up among the clothes.

Sir T. More, *The History of King Richard III.*

Strange it was thought, and absurd above the rest, to chase and keep out of the house *silly* swallows, harmless and gentle creatures.

Holland, *Plutarch's Morals*, p. 776.

SINCERE, SINCERITY. } The etymology of 'sincerus' being uncertain, it is impossible to say what is the primary notion of our English 'sincere.' It and 'sincerity' no less belong now to an ethical sphere exclusively; but the absence of foreign admixture which they predicate might be literal once.

The mind of a man, as it is not of that content or receipt to comprehend knowledge without helps and supplies, so again, it is not *sincere*, but of an ill and corrupt tincture.

Bacon, *Of the Interpretation of Nature*, c. xvi.

The Germans are a people that more than all the world, I think, may boast *sincerity*, as being for some thousands of years a pure and unmixed people.

Feltham, *A brief Character of the Low Countries*, p. 59.

SKELETON. Now the complex of bones as entirely denuded of the flesh; but in early English, and there in stricter agreement with its etymology, the *dried* mummy.

Scelet; the dead body of a man artificially dried or tanned for to be kept or seen a long time.

Holland, *Plutarch's Morals; An Explanation of certain obscure Words.*

SOFT,
SOFTNESS. } It is not an honorable fact that 'soft' and 'softness' should now be terms of slight, almost of contempt, when ethically employed; although indeed it is only a repetition of what we find in χρηστός, εὐήθης, 'gutig,' 'bonhomie,' and other words not a few.

That they speak evil of no man, that they be no fighters, but *soft* [ἐπιεικεῖς], showing all meekness unto all men.

Titus iii. 2. Tyndale.

The meek or *soft* shall inherit the earth; even as we say, Be still, and have thy will.

Tyndale, *Exposition on the v., vi., vii. Chapters of St. Matthew.*

Let your *softness* [τὸ ἐπιεικὲς ὑμῶν] be known unto all men.

Phil. iv. 5. Cranmer.

SONNET. A 'sonnet' now must consist of exactly fourteen lines, neither more nor less; and these with a fixed arrangement, though admitting a certain relaxation, of the rhymes; but 'sonnet' used often to be applied to *any* shorter poem, especially of an amatory kind.

He [Arion] had a wonderful desire to chaunt a *sonnet* or hymn unto Apollo Pythius.

Holland, *Plutarch's Morals*, p. 343.

If ye will tell us a tale, or play a jig, or show us a play and fine sights, or sing *sonnets* in our ears, there we will be for you.

Rogers, *Naaman the Syrian*, p. 492.

SOT, SOTTISH, SOTTISHNESS. He only is a 'sot' now whose stupor and folly is connected with, and the result of, excessive drink. But *any* fool would once bear this name.

In Egypt oft has seen the *sot* bow down,
And reverence some deified baboon.

Oldham, *The Eighth Satire of Boileau.*

He [Perseus] commanded those poor divers to be secretly murdered, that no person should remain alive that was privy to that *sottish* commandment of his.

Holland, *Livy*, p. 1177.

A leper once he lost, and gained a king,
Ahaz his *sottish* conqueror, whom he drew
God's altar to disparage and displace
For one of Syrian mode.

Milton, *Paradise Lost*, b. i.

Sottishness and dotage is the extinguishing of reason in phlegm or cold.

H. More, *The Grand Mystery of Godliness*, b. viii. c. 14.

SPARKLE. Water 'sparkles' most when it is *scattered*. This must explain the transition of the word from its former meaning, as indicated in the passages given below, to its present.

The Lansgrave hath *sparkled* his army without any further enterprise.

State Papers, vol. x. p. 718.

And awhile chawing all those things in his mouth, he spitteth it upon him whom he desireth to kill; who being *sparkled* therewith, dieth by force of the poison within the space of half an hour.

Purchas's Pilgrims, part ii. p. 1495.

SPECIOUS. Like the Latin 'speciosus' it simply signified beautiful once; it now means always, presenting a deceitful appearance of that beauty which is not really possessed, and is never used in any but an ethical sense.

> This prince hadde a dowter dere, Asneth was her name,
> A virgine ful *specious*, and semely of stature.
>
> *Metrical Romance of the Fourteenth Century.*

> Which [almug-trees], if odoriferous, made that passage as sweet to the smell as *specious* to the sight.
>
> Fuller, *A Pisgah Sight of Palestine*, b. iii. c. 2. § 5.

SPICE. We have in English a double adoption of the Latin 'species,' namely 'spice' and 'species.' 'Spice,' the earlier form in which we made the word our own, is now limited to aromatic drugs, which, as consisting of various *kinds*, have this name of 'spices.' But 'spice' was once employed as 'species' is now.

> Absteyne you fro al yvel *spice* [ab omni *specie* malâ, Vulg.].
>
> 1 *Thess.* v. 22. Wiclif.

> The *spices* of penance ben three. That oñ of hem is solempne, another is commune, and the thridde privie.
>
> Chaucer, *The Persones Tale.*

> Justice, although it be but one entire virtue, yet is described in two kinds of *spices*. The one is named justice distributive, the other is called commutative.
>
> Sir T. Elyot, *The Governor*, b. iii. c. 1.

SPINSTER. A name that used to be not uncommonly applied to women of evil life, in that they were set to enforced labor of spinning in the spittle or House of Correction, and thus were 'spinsters.' None of our Dictionaries, so far as I have observed, take note of this use of the word.

Many would never be indicted *spinsters*, were they spinsters indeed, nor come to so public and shameful punishments, if painfully employed in that vocation.

Fuller, *The Worthies of England, Kent.*

Geta. These women are still troublesome;
There be houses provided for such wretched women,
And some small rents to set ye a spinning.
Drusilla. Sir,
We are no *spinsters*, nor, if you look upon us,
So wretched as you take us.

Beaumont and Fletcher, *The Prophetess,* Act iii. Sc. 1.

STAPLE. A curious change has come over this word. We should now say, Cotton is the great 'staple,' that is, the established merchandize, of Manchester; our fathers would have reversed this and said, Manchester is the great 'staple' or established mart of cotton. We make the goods prepared or sold, the 'staple of the place, they made the place the 'staple' of the goods.

Men in all ages have made themselves merry with singling out some place, and fixing the *staple* of stupidity and stolidity therein.

Fuller, *The Worthies of England, Nottinghamshire.*

Staple; a city or town, where merchants jointly lay up their commodities for the better uttering of them by the great; a public storehouse.

Phillips, *The New World of Words.*

Starve. The Anglo-Saxon 'steorfan,' the German 'sterben,' to die, it is only by comparatively modern use restricted to perishing *by cold or by hunger;* in this restriction of use, resembling somewhat the French 'noyer,' to kill *by drowning*, while 'necare,' from which it descends, is to kill by any manner of death. But innumerable words are thus like rivers, which once pouring their waters through many channels, have now left dry land and abandoned them all, save one, or as in the present instance it happens, save two.

> For wele or wo she n'ill him not forsake:
> She n'is not wery him to love and serve,
> Though that he lie bedrede til that he *sterve.*
>
> Chaucer, *The Merchantes Tale.*

> But, if for me ye fight, or me will serve,
> Not this rude kind of battle, nor these arms
> Are meet, the which do men in bale to *sterve.*
>
> Spenser, *The Fairy Queen*, ii. 6, 34.

State. Used often by our old writers for a raised dais or platform, on which was placed a chair or throne with a canopy (the German 'Thronhimmel') above it; being the chiefest seat of honor; thus in Massinger's *Bondman*, Act i. Sc. 3, according to the old stage-direction Archidamus "offers Timoleon the *state.*"

> But for a canopy to shade her head,
> No *state* which lasts no longer than 'tis stayed,
> And fastened up by cords and pillars' aid.
>
> Beaumont, *Psyche*, can. xix. st. 170.

Their majesties were seated as is aforesaid under their canopies or *states*, whereof that of the Queen was somewhat lesser and lower than that of the King, but both of them exceeding rich.

History of the Coronation of King James II., 1687, p. 61.

When he went to court, he used to kick away the *state*, and sit down by his prince cheek by jowl. Confound these *states*, says he, they are a modern invention.

Swift, *History of John Bull*, part ii. c. 1.

STATIONER. There was a time when 'stationer,' meaning properly no more than one who had his *station*, that is, in the market-place or elsewhere, included the bookseller and the publisher as well as the dealer in the raw material of books. But when, in the division of labor, these became separate businesses, the name was restrained to him who dealt in the latter articles alone.

I doubt not but that the Animadvertor's *stationer* doth hope and desire that he hath thus pleased people in his book, for the advancing of the price and quickening the sale thereof.

Fuller, *The Appeal of Injured Innocence*, p. 38.

The right of the printed copies (which the *stationer* takes as his own freehold) was dispersed in five or six several hands.

Oley, *Preface to Dr. Jackson's Works.*

STICKLE, STICKLER. Now to stand with a certain pertinacity to one's point, refusing to renounce or go back from it; but formerly equivalent to the emphatic 'décharpir,' a word which the French language has now let go, to interpose between combatants and separate them, when they had sufficiently satisfied the laws of honor; some deriving it from the wands, sceptres, or *sticks* with which the heralds engaged in this office separated the combatants. Our present meaning of the word connects itself with the past in the fact that the 'sticklers, or seconds, as we should call them now, often fulfilled another function, being ready to maintain in their own persons and by their own arms the quarrel of their principals, and thus to 'stickle' for it.

> Betwixt which three a question grew,
> Which should the worthiest be;
> Which violently they pursue,
> And would not *stickled* be.
>
> Drayton, *Muses' Elysium, Nymph.* 6.

The same angel [in Tasso], when half of the Christians are already killed, and all the rest are in a fair way of being routed, *stickles* betwixt the remainders of God's hosts and the race of fiends; pulls the devils backwards by the tails, and drives them from their quarry.

Dryden, *Dedication of Translations from Juvenal*, p. 122.

> The dragon wing of night o'erspreads the earth,
> And, *stickler*-like, the armies separates.
>
> Shakespeare, *Troilus and Cressida*, Act v. Sc. 9.

> Our former chiefs, like *sticklers* of the war,
> First fought to inflame the parties, then to poise;
> The quarrel loved, but did the cause abhor,
> And did not strike to hurt, but make a noise.
>
> Dryden, *On the Death of Oliver Cromwell.*

STOUT, STOUTNESS. The temptation to the strong to be also the proud is so natural, so difficult to resist, and resisted by so few, that it is nothing wonderful when words, first meaning the one, pass over into the sense of the other. 'Stout,' however, has not retained, except in some provincial use, the sense of proud, nor 'stoutness' of pride.

For had not Eumenes been so ambitious and *stout* to strive against Antigonus for the chiefest place of authority, but could have been contented with the second, Antigonus would have been right glad thereof.

North, *Plutarch's Lives*, p. 509.

Come all to ruin; let
Thy mother rather feel thy pride, than fear
Thy dangerous *stoutness;* for I mock at death
With as big heart as thou.

Shakespeare, *Coriolanus*, Act iii. Sc. 2.

STOVE. This word has much narrowed its meaning. Bath, hothouse, any room where air or water were artificially heated, was a 'stove' once.

When a certain Frenchman came to visit Melancthon, he found him in his *stove*, with one hand dandling his child in the swaddling-clouts, and the other holding a book and reading it.

Fuller, *The Holy State*, b. ii. c. 9.

How tedious is it to them that live in *stoves* and caves half a year together, as in Iceland, Muscovy, or under the pole!

Burton, *The Anatomy of Melancholy*, part i. sect. 2.

SUBLIME. There is an occasional use of 'sublime' by our earlier poets, a use in which it bears much the meaning of the Greek ὑπερήφανος, or perhaps approaches still more closely to that of μετέωρος, high and lifted up as with pride; which has now quite departed from it.

For the proud Soldan with presumptuous cheer,
And countenance *sublime* and insolent,
Sought only slaughter and avengément.

Spenser, *The Fairy Queen*, b. v. c. 8.

Their hearts were jocund and *sublime*,
Drunk with idolatry, drunk with wine.

Milton, *Samson Agonistes*.

SURE. Used once in the sense of affianced, or 'hand-fasted.' See 'ASSURE,' 'ENSURE.'

The king was *sure* to dame Elizabeth Lucy, and her husband before God.

Sir T. More, *The History of King Richard III.*

SUSPECT, SUSPICION. To 'suspect' is properly to look under, and out of this fact is derived our present use of the word; but in looking *under* you may also look *up*, and herein lies the explanation of an occasional use of 'suspect' and 'suspicion' which we find in our early writers.

Pelopidas being sent the second time into Thessaly, to make accord betwixt the people and Alexander, the tyrant of Pheres, was by this tyrant (not *suspecting* the dignity of an ambassador, nor of his country) made prisoner.

North, *Plutarch's Lives*, p. 927.

If God do intimate to the spirit of any wise inferiors that they ought to reprove, then let them *suspect* their own persons, and beware that they make no open contestation, but be content with privacy.

Rogers, *Naaman the Syrian*, p. 330.

Cordeilla out of mere love, without the *suspicion* of expected reward, at the message only of her father in distress, pours forth true filial tears.

Milton, *The History of England*, b. i.

Sycophant. The early meaning of 'sycophant,' when it was employed as equivalent to informer, delator, calumniator, 'promoter,' agreed better with its assumed derivation, and undoubted use, in the Greek, than does our present. Employing it as we now do in the sense of false and fawning flatterer, we might seem at first sight to employ it in a sense not merely altogether unconnected with, but quite opposite to, its former. Yet indeed there is a very deep inner connection between the two uses. It is not for nothing that Jeremy Taylor treats of these two, "Of Slander and Flattery," in one and the same sermon.

The poor man that hath nought to lose is not afraid of the *sycophant* or promoter.

Holland, *Plutarch's Morals*, p. 261.

He [St. Paul] in peril of the wilderness, that is of wild beasts; they [rich men] not only of the wild beast called the *sycophant*, but of the tame beast too, called the flatterer.

Andrews, *Sermon preached at the Spittle.*

Sanders, that malicious *sycophant*, will have no less than twenty-six wain-load of silver, gold, and precious stones to be seized into the king's hands by the spoil of that monument.

Heylin, *The History of the Reformation*, ed. 1849, vol. i. p. 20.

Symbol. The employment of 'symbol' in its proper Greek sense of contribution thrown into a common stock, as in a pic-nic, or the like, is frequent in Jeremy Taylor, and examples of it may be found in other scholarly writers of the seventeenth century.

The consideration of these things hath oft suggested, and at length persuaded me to make this attempt, to cast in my mite to this treasury, my *symbolum* toward so charitable a work.

Hammond, *A Paraphrase and Annotations on the Psalms, Preface.*

Christ hath finished his own sufferings for expiation of the world; yet there are "portions that are behind of the sufferings" of Christ, which must be filled up by his body the Church; and happy are they that put in the greatest *symbol*; for "in the same measure you are partakers of the sufferings of Christ, in the same shall ye be also of the consolation."

J. Taylor, *The Faith and Patience of the Saints.*

T.

TABLE. The Latin 'tabula' had for one of its meanings picture or painting; and this caused that 'table' was by our early writers used often in the same meaning.

The *table* wherein Detraction was expressed, he [Apelles] painted in this form.

Sir T. Elyot, *The Governor*, b. iii. c. 27.

You shall see, as it were in a *table* painted before your eyes, the evil-favouredness and deformity of this most detestable vice.

Homilies; Sermon against Contention.

Learning flourished yet in the city of Sicyon, and they esteemed the painting of *tables* in that city to be the perfectest for true colours and fine drawing, of all other places.

North, *Plutarch's Lives*, p. 843.

TALL. Our ancestors superinduced on the primary meaning of 'tall' a secondary, resting on the assumption that tall men would be also brave, and this often with a dropping of the notion of height altogether.

His [the Earl of Richmond's] companions being almost in despair of victory were suddenly recomforted by Sir William Stanley, which came to succours with three thousand *tall* men.

Grafton, *Chronicle.*

Tamburlaine. Where are my common soldiers now, that fought
So lionlike upon Asphaltis' plains?
Soldier. Here, my lord.
Tamburlaine. Hold ye, *tall* soldiers, take ye queens apiece.

Marlowe, *Tamburlaine the Great,* part ii., Act iv. Sc. 4.

He [Prince Edward] would proffer to fight with any mean person, if cried up by the volge for a *tall* man.

Fuller, *The Holy War,* b. iv. c. 29.

TARPAULIN. Not any longer used except in the shorter form of 'tar' for sailor.

The Archbishop of Bourdeaux is at present General of the French naval forces, who though a priest, is yet permitted to turn *tarpaulin* and soldier.

The Turkish Spy, Letter 2.

TEMPER. What has been said under the word 'humour' will also explain 'temper,' and the earlier uses of it which we meet. The happy 'temper' would be the happy mixture, the blending in due proportions, of the four principal 'humours' of the body.

The exquisiteness of his [the Saviour's] bodily *temper* increased the exquisiteness of his torment, and the ingenuity of his soul added to his sensibleness of the indignities and affronts offered to him.

Fuller, *A Pisgah Sight of Palestine*, vol. i. p. 345.

Concupiscence itself follows the crasis and temperature of the body. If you would know why one man is proud, another cruel, another intemperate or luxurious, you are not to repair so much to Aristotle's ethics, or to the writings of other moralists, as to those of Galen, or of some anatomists, to find the reason of these different *tempers*.

South, *Sermons*, 1744, vol. ii. p. 5.

Temperament. The Latin 'temperamentum' has sometimes very nearly the sense of our English 'compromise,' signifying, as this does, a middle term reached by mutual concession, by a *tempering* of the extreme claims upon either side. I am indisposed to think that the use of 'temperament' in this same meaning is peculiar to Milton, though I have no second example at hand.

Safest, therefore, to me it seems that none of the Council be moved unless by death, or just conviction of some crime. However, I forejudge not any probable expedient, any *temperament* that can be found in things of this nature, so disputable on either side.

Milton, *The Ready and Easy Way to establish a Free Commonwealth.*

Termagant. This would now be applied only to *females* of fierce temper and ungoverned tongue, but formerly to male and female alike; and indeed predominantly to the first.

Art thou so fierce, currish, and churlish a Nabal, that even when thou mightest live in the midst of thy people (as she told Elisha [2 *Kings* iv. 13]), thou delightest to play the tyrant and *termagant* among them?

Rogers, *Naaman the Syrian*, p. 270.

THEWS. It is a remarkable evidence of Shakespeare's influence upon the English language, that while, so far as yet has been observed, every other writer, one single instance excepted, employs 'thews' in the sense of manners, qualities of mind and disposition, the fact that, as often as he employs it, it is in the sense of nerves, muscular vigor, has quite overborne the other use; which, once so familiar in our literature, has now quite passed away. See a valuable note in Craik's *English of Shakespeare*, p. 117.

To all good *thewes* born was she;
As liked to the goddes or she was born,
That of the shefe she should be the corne.

Chaucer, *The Legend of Hypermestre.*

For every thing to which one is inclined
Doth best become and greatest grace doth gain;
Yet praise likewise deserve good *thewes* enforced with pain.

Spenser, *The Fairy Queen*, b. ii. 2.

THOUGHT. Many, as they read or hear in our English Bible these words of our Lord, "Take no *thought* for your life" (*Matt.* vi. 25), are perplexed, for they can not help thinking that there is some exaggeration in them, that He is urging here something which is impossible, and which, if possible, would not be desirable, but a forfeiting of the true dignity of man. Or, perhaps, if they are able to compare the English with the Greek, they blame our Translators for having given an emphasis to the precept which it did not possess in the original. But neither is the fact. 'Thought' is constantly *anxious* care in our earlier English, as the examples which follow will abundantly prove.

He so plagued and vexed his father with injurious indignities, that the old man for very *thought* and grief of heart pined away and died.

Holland, *Camden's Ireland*, p. 120.

In five hundred years only two queens have died in childbirth. Queen Catherine Parr died rather of *thought*.

Tracts during the Reign of Queen Elizabeth; Somers Tracts, vol. i. p. 172.

Harris, an alderman of London, was put in trouble, and died of *thought* and anxiety before his business came to an end.

Bacon, *The History of King Henry VII.*

THRIFTY. The 'thrifty' is on the way to be the thriving; yet 'thrifty' does not mean thriving now, as once it did. It still indeed retains this meaning in provincial use, as I have heard a newly-transplanted tree which was doing well, described as 'thrifty.'

No grace hath more abundant promises made unto it than this of mercy, a sowing, a reaping, a *thrifty* grace.

Bishop Reynolds, *Sermon* 30.

TINSEL. This is always now *cheap* finery, glistening like silver and gold, but at the same time pretending a value and a richness which it does not really possess. There was no such habitual insinuation of pretentious finery in its earlier uses.

Every place was hanged with cloth of gold, cloth of silver, *tinsel*, arras, tapestry, and what not.

Stubs, *The Anatomy of Abuses*, p. 18.

[He] never cared for silks or sumptuous cost,
For cloth of gold, or *tinsel* figurie,
For baudkin, broidery, cutworks, nor conceits.

Gascoigne, *The Steel Glass.*

TOBACCONIST. Now the seller, once the smoker, of tobacco.

Germany hath not so many drunkards, England *tobacconists*, France dancers, Holland mariners, as Italy alone hath jealous husbands.

Burton, *The Anatomy of Melancholy*, part iii. sect. 3.

But let it be of any truly said,
He's great, religious, learned, wise or staid,
But he is lately turned *tobacconist*,
Oh what a blur! what an abatement is't!

Sylvester, *Tobacco Battered.*

TORY. It is curious how often political parties have ended by assuming to themselves names first fastened on them by their adversaries in reproach and scorn. The 'Gueux' or 'Beggars' of Holland are perhaps the most notable instance of all; so too 'tories' was a name properly belonging to the Irish bogtrotters, who during our Civil Wars robbed and plundered, professing to be in arms for the maintenance of the royal cause; and from them transferred, about the year 1680, to those who sought to maintain the extreme prerogatives of the Crown.

Mosstroopers, a sort of rebels in the northern part of Scotland, that live by robbery and spoil, like the *tories* in Ireland, or the banditi in Italy.

Phillips, *The New World of Words*, ed. 1706.

TREACLE. At present it means only the sweet syrup of molasses, but a word once of far wider reach and far nobler significance, having come to us from afar, and by steps which are curious to be traced. They are these: the Greeks, in anticipation of modern homœopathy, called a supposed antidote to the viper's bite, which was composed of the viper's flesh, θηριακή, from θηρίον, a name often given to the viper *(Acts* xxviii. 5); of this came the Latin 'theriaca,' and our 'theriac,' of which, or rather of the Latin form, 'treacle' is but a popular corruption.

For a most strong *treacle* against these venomous heresies wrought our Saviour many a marvellous miracle.

Sir T. More, *A Treatise on the Passion, Works*, p. 1357.

At last his body [Sir Thomas Overbury's] was almost come by use of poisons to the state that Mithridates' body was by the use of *treacle* and preservatives, that the force of the poisons was blunted upon him.

Bacon, *Charge against Robert, Earl of Somerset.*

The saints' experiences help them to a sovereign *treacle* made of the scorpion's own flesh (which they through Christ have slain), and that hath a virtue above all other to expel the venom of Satan's temptations from the heart.

Gurnall, *The Christian in Complete Armour*, c. ix. § 2.

Treacle; a physical composition, made of vipers and other ingredients.

Phillips, *The New World of Words.*

TRIUMPH. A name often transferred by our early writers to any stately shows and pageantries whatever, not restricted, as now, to those which celebrate a victory. See Lord Bacon's Essay, the 37th, with the heading, Of Masks and *Triumphs*, passim.

> Our daughter,
> In honour of whose birth these *triumphs* are,
> Sits here, like beauty's child.

Pericles, Prince of Tyre, Act ii. Sc. 2.

You cannot have a perfect palace except you have two several sides, the one for feasts and *triumphs,* the other for dwelling.

Bacon, *Essays,* 45.

TRIVIAL. A 'trivial' saying is at present a slight one; it was formerly a well-worn or often-repeated one, or, as we should now say, one that was trite; but this, it might be, on the ground of the weight and wisdom which it contained; as certainly the maxim quoted by Hacket is any thing but 'trivial' in our sense of the word. Gradually the notion of slightness was superadded to that of commonness, and thus an epithet once of honor has become one of dishonor rather.

Others avouch, and that more truly, that he [Duns Scotus] was born in Downe, and thereof they guess him to be named Dunensis, and by contraction Duns, which term is so *trivial* and common in the schools, that whoso surpasseth others either in cavilling sophistry or subtle philosophy is forthwith nicknamed a Duns.

Stanyhurst, *The Description of Ireland*, p. 2.

Æquitas optimo cuique notissima, is a *trivial* saying, A very good man cannot be ignorant of equity.

Hacket, *The Life of Archbishop Williams*, part i. p. 57.

These branches [of the divine life] are three, whose names though *trivial* and vulgar, yet, if rightly understood, they bear such a sense with them, that nothing more weighty can be pronounced by the tongue of men or seraphims, and in brief they are these, Charity, Humility, and Purity.

H. More, *The Grand Mystery of Godliness*, b. ii. c. 12.

Trumpery. That which is deceitful is without any worth; and 'trumpery,' which was at first deceit, fraud (tromperie), is now any thing which is worthless and vile.

When truth appeared, Rogero hated more
Alcyna's *trumperies*, and did them detest,
Than he was late enamoured before.

Sir J. Harington, *Orlando Furioso*, b. vii.

Britannicus was now grown to man's estate, a true and worthy plant to receive his father's empire; which a grafted son by adoption now possessed by the injury and *trumpery* of his mother.

Greenway, *Tacitus*, p. 182.

Tuition. One defends another most effectually who imparts to him those principles and that knowledge whereby he shall be able to defend himself; and therefore our modern use of 'tuition' as teaching is a deeper one than the earlier, which made it to mean external rather than this internal protection.

As though they were not to be trusted with the king's brother, that by the assent of the nobles of the land were appointed, as the king's nearest friends, to the *tuition* of his own royal person.

Sir T. More, *The History of King Richard III.*, p. 36.

Afterwards turning his speech to his wife and son, he [Scanderbeg] commended them both with his kingdom to the *tuition* of the Venetians.

Knolles, *The History of the Turks*, vol. i. p. 274.

TURK. It is a remarkable evidence of the extent to which the Turks and the Turkish assault upon Christendom had impressed themselves on the minds of men, of the way in which they stood as representing the entire Mahometan world, that 'Turk,' being in fact a national, is constantly employed by the writers of the sixteenth and seventeenth centuries as a religious, designation, as equivalent to, and coextensive with, Mahometan; exactly as Ἕλλην in the New Testament means continually not Greek, but Gentile.

Have mercy upon all Jews, *Turks*, infidels, and Heretics.

Collect for Good Friday.

It is no good reason for a man's religion, that he was born and brought up in it; for then a *Turk* would have as much reason to be a *Turk* as a Christian to be a Christian.

Chillingworth, *The Religion of Protestants a safe Way unto Salvation*, part i. c. 2.

U.

UMBRAGE, UMBRAGEOUS. 'To take umbrage' is, I think, the only phrase in which the word 'umbrage' is still in use among us, the only one at least in which it is ethically employed; but 'umbrage' in its earlier use coincides in meaning with the old French 'ombrage' (see the quotation from Bacon), and signifies suspicion, or rather the disposition to suspect; and 'umbrageous,' as far as I know, is constantly employed in the sense of suspicious by our early authors; having now no other but a literal sense. Other uses of 'umbrage,' as those of Fuller and Jeremy Taylor which follow, must be explained from the classical sympathies of these writers; out of which the Latin etymology of the word gradually made itself felt in the meaning which they ascribed to it, namely, as any thing slight and *shadowy*.

I say, just fear, not out of *umbrages*, light jealousies, apprehensions afar off, but out of clear foresight of imminent danger.

Bacon, *Of a War with Spain.*

To collect the several essays of princes glancing on that project [a new Crusade], were a task of great pains and small profit; especially some of them being *umbrages* and state representations rather than realities, to ingratiate princes with their subjects, or with the oratory of so pious a project to woo money out of people's purses.

Fuller, *The Holy War*, b. v. c. 25.

You look for it [truth] in your books, and you tug hard for it in your disputations, and you derive it from the cisterns of the Fathers, and you inquire after the old ways; and sometimes are taken with new appearances, and you rejoice in false lights, or are delighted with little *umbrages* or peep of day.

J. Taylor, *A Sermon preached to the University of Dublin.*

At the beginning some men were a little *umbrageous*, and startling at the name of the Fathers; yet since the Fathers have been well studied, we have behaved ourselves with more reverence toward the Fathers than they of the Roman persuasion have done.

Donne, *Sermons*, 1640, p. 557.

That there was none other present but himself when his master De Merson was murdered, it is *umbrageous*, and leaves a spice of fear and sting of suspicion in their heads.

Reynolds, *God's Revenge against Murder*, b. iii. hist. 13.

UNCOUTH. Now unformed in manner, ungraceful in behavior; but once simply unknown. The change in signification is to be traced to the same causes which made 'barbarous,' meaning at first only foreign, to have afterwards the sense of savage and wild. Almost all nations regard with disfavor and dislike that which is outlandish, and generally that with which they are unacquainted; so that words which at first did but express this fact of strangeness, easily acquire a further unfavorable sense.

The vulgar instruction requires also vulgar and communicable terms, not clerkly or *uncouth*, as are all these of the Greek and Latin languages.

Puttenham, *The Art of English Poesy*, b. iii. c. 10.

Wel-away the while I was so fond,
To leave the good that I had in hond,
In hope of better that was *uncouth;*
So lost the dog the flesh in his mouth.

Spenser, *The Shepherd's Calendar, September.*

"*Uncouth*, unkist," said the old famous poet, Chaucer; which proverb very well taketh place in this our new poet, who for that he is *uncouth* (as said Chaucer) is unkist; and, *unknown* to most men, is regarded but of a few.

E. K., *Epistle Dedicatory prefixed to Spenser's Shepherd's Calendar.*

UNEQUAL. From the constant use made of 'unequal' by our early writers, for whom it was entirely equivalent to unjust, unfair, one might almost suppose they saw in it 'iniquus' rather than 'inæqualis.' At any rate they had no scruple in using it in this sense, which 'inæqualis' never has, but 'iniquus' continually.

Is not my way *equal?* are not your ways *unequal?*

Ezek. xviii. 25. Authorized Version.

These imputations are too common, sir,
And easily stuck on virtue, when she's poor:
You are *unequal* to me.

Ben Jonson, *The Fox*, Act iii. Sc. 1.

Jerome, a very *unequal* relator of the opinion of his adversaries.

Worthington, *The Life of Joseph Mede*, p. xi.

UNHANDSOME. See 'HANDSOME.'

A narrow straight path by the water's side, very *unhandsome* [οὐ ῥᾳδίαν] for an army to pass that way, though they found not a man to keep the passage.

North, *Plutarch's Lives*, p. 317.

The ships were unwieldy and *unhandsome*.

Holland, *Livy*, p. 1188.

UNKIND,
UNKINDNESS. } 'Unkind' has quite forfeited now its primary meaning, namely, that which violates the law of kind, thus "*unkind* abominations" (Chaucer), meaning incestuous unions and the like; and has taken up with the secondary, that which does not recognize the duties flowing out of this kinship. In its primary meaning it moves in a region where the physical and ethical meet; in its secondary in a purely ethical sphere. How soon it began to occupy this the passages which follow will show; for out of a sense that nothing was so unnatural or 'unkind' as ingratitude, it early obtained use as a special designation of this vice.

Unkynde [ingrati], cursid, withouten affeccioun.

2 *Tim.* iii. 2, 3. Wiclif.

It is all one to sey *unkinde*,
As thing whiche doone is againe kinde,
For it with kinde never stoode
A man to yelde evill for goode.

Gower, *Confessio Amantis*, b. v.

The most damnable vice and most against justice, in mine opinion, is ingratitude, commonly called *unkindness*. He is *unkind* that denieth to have received any benefit, that indeed he hath received; he is *unkind* that dissimuleth; he is *unkind* that recompenseth not; but he is most *unkind* that forgetteth.

Sir T. Elyot, *The Governor*, b. ii. c. 13.

UNHAPPY, UNHAPPINESS. A very deep truth lies involved in the fact that so many words, and I suppose in all languages, unite the meanings of wicked and miserable, as the Greek σχέτλος, our own 'wretch' and 'wretched.' So, too, it was once with 'unhappy,' although its use in the sense of 'wicked' has now passed away.

Fathers shall do well also to keep from them [their children] such schoolfellows as be *unhappy*, and given to shrewd turns; for such as they are enough to corrupt and mar the best natures in the world.

Holland, *Plutarch's Morals*, p. 16.

Thou old *unhappy* traitor,
Briefly thyself remember; the sword is out
That must destroy thee.

Shakespeare, *King Lear*, Act iv. Sc. 6.

The servants of Dionyse, king of Sicily, which although they were inclined to all *unhappiness* and mischief, yet after the coming of Plato, perceiving that for his doctrine and wisdom the king had him in high estimation, they thus counterfeited the countenance and habit of the philosopher.

Sir T. Elyot, *The Governor*, b. ii. c. 14.

[Man] from the hour of his birth is most miserable, weak, and sickly; when he sucks, he is guided by others; when he is grown great, practiseth *unhappiness* and is sturdy; and when old, a child again and repenteth him of his past life.

Burton, *The Anatomy of Melancholy*; *Democritus to the Reader*.

UNION. The elder Pliny (*H. N.* ix. 59) tells us that the name 'unio' had not very long before his time begun to be given to a pearl in which all chiefest excellencies, size, roundness, smoothness, whiteness, weight met and, so to speak, were *united;* and as late as Jeremy Taylor the word 'union' was often employed by our best writers in this sense, namely, that of a pearl of a rare and transcendent beauty.

And in the cup an *union* shall he throw,
Richer than that which four successive kings
In Denmark's crown have worn.

Shakespeare, *Hamlet*, Act v. Sc. 2

Pope Paul II. in his pontifical vestments outwent all his predecessors, especially in his mitre, upon which he had laid out a great deal of money in purchasing at vast rates diamonds, sapphires, emeralds, crysoliths, jaspers, *unions*, and all manner of precious stones.

Sir Paul Rycaut, *Platina's History of the Popes*, p. 114.

Perox, the Persian king, [hath] an *union* in his ear worth an hundred weight of gold.

Burton, *The Anatomy of Melancholy*, mem. ii. sect. 3.

USURY, USURER. This, which is now the lending of money upon inordinate interest, was once the lending it upon any. The man who did not lend his money for nothing was then a 'usurer,' not he, as now, who makes unworthy profit by the necessities of the needy or the extravagance of the foolish. It is true that the word was as dishonorable then as it is now; and it could not be otherwise, so long as all receiving of interest was regarded as a violation at once of divine and of natural law. When at length the common sense of men overcame this strange but deep-rooted prejudice, the word was too deeply stained with dishonor to be employed to express the lawful receiving of a measurable interest; but 'usury,' taking up a portion only of its former meaning, was now restricted to that which still remained under a moral ban, namely, the exacting of an excessive interest for money lent.

On the other side, the commodities of *usury* are: first, that howsoever *usury* in some respect hindereth merchandizing, yet in some other it advanceth it; for it is certain that the greatest part of trade is driven by young merchants upon *borrowing at interest;* so as if the *usurer* either call in or keep back his money, there will ensue presently a great stand of trade.

Bacon, *Essays.*

Wherefore then gavest not thou my money into the bank, that at my coming I might have required mine own with *usury* [σὺν τόκῳ]?

Luke xix. 23. Authorized Version.

Brokers, takers of pawns, biting *usurers* I will not admit; yet because we converse here with men, not with gods, and for the hardness of men's hearts, I will tolerate some kind of *usury.*

Burton, *The Anatomy of Melancholy; Democritus to the Reader.*

UNTHRIFTY, UNTHRIFTINESS. As the 'thrifty' will probably be the thriving, so the 'unthrifty' the unthriving; but the words are not synonymous any more, as once they were.

What [is it] but this self and presuming of ourselves causes grace to be *unthrifty,* and to hang down the head; what but our ascribing to ourselves in our means-using, makes them so unfruitful?

Rogers, *Naaman the Syrian,* p. 146.

Staggering, non-proficiency, and *unthriftiness* of profession is the fruit of self.

Id., *Index.*

UNVALUED. This and 'invaluable' have been usefully desynonymized; so that 'invaluable' means now having a value greater than can be estimated, 'unvalued' esteemed to have no value at all.

Two golden apples of *unvalued* price.

Spenser, *Sonnet* 77.

Go, *unvalued* book,
Live, and be loved; if any envious look
Hurt thy clear fame, learn that no state more high
Attends on virtue than pined envy's eye.

Chapman, *Dedication of Poems.*

Each heart
Hath from the leaves of thy *unvalued* book
Those Delphic lines with deep impression took.
Milton, *An Epitaph on Shakespeare.*

V.

VERMIN. Now always noxious offensive animals of the *smaller* kind; but employed formerly with no such limitation.

This crocodile is a mischievous four-footed beast, a dangerous *vermin* used to both elements.
Holland, *Ammianus*, p. 212.

Wherein were all manner of four-footed beasts of the earth, and *vermin* [καὶ τὰ θηρία], and worms, and fowls of the air.
Acts x. 12. Geneva.

The Lord rectifies Peter, and frames him to go by a vision of all crawling *vermin* in a clean sheet.
Rogers, *Naaman the Syrian*, p. 42.

VILLAIN, VILLANY. A word of which the story is so well known that one may be spared the necessity of repeating it. It was, I think, with 'villany' that there was first a transfer into an ethical sphere, though it is very noticeable how 'villany' till a very late day expressed *words* of infamy much oftener than *deeds*.

Pour the blood of the *villain* in one basin, and the blood of the gentleman in another; what difference shall here be proved?
Becon, *The Jewel of Joy.*

We yield not ourselves to be your *villains* and slaves [non in servitutem nos tradimus], but as allies to be protected by you.

Holland, *Livy*, p. 935.

[He] was condemned to be degraded of all nobility, and not only himself, but all his succeeding posterity declared *villains* and clowns, taxable and incapable to bear arms.

Florio, *Essays of Montaigne*, b. i. c. 15.

In our modern language it [foul language] is termed *villany*, as being proper for rustic boors, or men of coarsest education and employment, who, having their minds debased by being conversant in meanest affairs, do vent their sorry passions in such strains.

Barrow, *Of Evil-speaking in general*, Sermon 16.

Vivacious, Vivacity. 'Longevity,' as one might expect to find it, is a comparatively modern word in the language. 'Vivacity,' which has now acquired the mitigated sense of liveliness, served instead of it; keeping in English the original sense which 'vivacitas' had in the Latin.

James Sands, of Horborn in this county, is most remarkable for his *vivacity*, for he lived 140 years.

Fuller, *The Worthies of England, Staffordshire.*

Hitherto the English bishops had been *vivacious* almost to wonder. For, necessarily presumed of good years before entering on their office in the first year of Queen Elizabeth, it was much that but five died for the first twenty years of her reign.

Id., *The Church History of Britain*, b. ix. § 27.

Voluble. This epithet always insinuates of him to whom it is applied now that his speech is freer and faster than is meet; but it once occupied that region of meaning which 'fluent' does at present, without any suggestion of the kind.

He [Archbishop Abbott] was painful, stout, severe against bad manners, of a grave and a *voluble* eloquence.

Hacket, *The Life of Archbishop Williams*, part i. p. 65.

W.

WAINSCOT. This was very commonly restrained to *oaken* timber or *oaken* boarding alone.

A wedge of *wainscot* is fittest and most proper for cleaving of an *oaken* tree.

Sir T. Urquhart, *Tracts*, p. 153.

Being thus arrayed, and enclosed in a chest of *wainscot*, he [Edward the Confessor] was removed into the before-prepared feretry.

Dart, *History of St. Peter's, Westminster*, b. ii. c. 3.

WHIRLPOOL. None of our Dictionaries, as far as I am aware, have noticed the use of 'whirlpool' to designate some huge sea-monster of the whale kind.

The Indian Sea breedeth the most and the biggest fishes that are; among which the whales and *whirlpools*, called balænæ, take up in length as much as four acres or arpens of land.

Holland, *Pliny*, vol i. p. 235.

The ork, *whirlpool*, whale, or huffing physeter.

Sylvester, *Du Bartas*, *First Day of the Week.*

WIGHT. The best discussion on this interesting word is to be found in Grimm's *Deutsche Mythologie*, pp. 408–410, who has a chapter, On Wights and Elves. 'Wight' has lost altogether now with us its original sense of a preternatural or supernatural being, and is used, but always slightingly, of men. It is easy to see how, with the gradual contempt for the old mythology, the dying-out of the superstitions connected with it, the words of it, such as 'elf' and 'wight,' should have lost their weight and honor as well.

I crouche thee from elves and from *wights*.

Chaucer, *The Millers Tale.*

The poet Homer speaketh of no garlands and chaplets but due to the celestial and heavenly *wights*.

Holland, *Pliny*, vol. i. p. 456.

A black horse cometh, and his rider hath a balance, and a voice telleth among the four *wights* that corn shall be dear.

Broughton, *Of Consent upon Apocalypse.*

When the four *wights* are said to have given glory, honour, and thanks to Him that sate upon the throne [*Rev.* v. 14], what was their ditty but this?

Mede, *Sermons.*

WILFUL, WILFULLY. 'Wilful' and 'willing,' 'wilfully' and 'willingly,' have been conveniently desynonymized by later usage in our language; so that in 'wilful' and 'wilfully' there now lies ever the sense of will capriciously exerted, finding its motives merely in itself; while the examples which follow show there was once no such implication of *self*-will in the words.

Alle the sones of Israel halewiden *wilful* thingis to the Lord.

Exod. xxxv. 29. Wiclif.

Fede ye the flok of God, that is among you, and purvey ye, not as constreyned, but *wilfulli*.

1 *Pet.* v. 2. Wiclif.

And so, through his pitiful nailing, Christ shed out *wilfully* for man's life the blood that was in his veins.

Foxe, *The Book of Martyrs; Examination of William Thorpe.*

A proud priest may be known when he denieth to follow Christ and his apostles in *wilful* poverty and other virtues.

Id., *Ib.*

WINCE. Now to shrink or start away as in pain from a stroke or touch; but, as far as I know, used always by our earlier authors in the sense of to kick.

Poul, whom the Lord hadde chosun, long tyme *wynside* agen the pricke.

Wiclif, *Prolog on the Dedis of Apostlis.*

For this flower of age, having no forecaste of thrift, but set altogether upon spending, and given to delights and pleasures, *winseth* and flingeth out like a skittish and frampold horse in such sort that it had need of a sharp bit and short curb.

Holland, *Plutarch's Morals*, p. 14.

WIT, WITTY. The present meaning of 'wit' as compared with the past, and the period of transition from one to the other, can not be better marked than in the quotation from Bishop Reynolds which is given below.

Who knewe the *witte* of the Lord, or who was his counceilour?

Rom. xi. 34. Wiclif.

I take not *wit* in that common acceptation, whereby men understand some sudden flashes of conceit whether in style or conference, which, like rotten wood in the dark, have more shine than substance, whose use and ornament are, like themselves, swift and vanishing, at once both admired and forgotten. But I understand a settled, constant, and habitual sufficiency of the understanding, whereby it is enabled in any kind of learning, theory, or practice, both to sharpness in search, subtilty in expression, and despatch in execution.

Reynolds, *The Passions and Faculties of the Soul*, c. xxxix.

I confess notwithstanding, with the *wittiest* of the school-divines, that if we speak of strict justice God could no way have been bound to requite man's labours in so large and ample manner.

Hooker, *Ecclesiastical Polity*, b. i. c. 11.

Rare epicures and gluttons, fit to be presidents of a Greek symposiac, not for their skill in philosophy, but their *witty* arts of drinking.

J. Taylor, *The Doctrine and Practice of Repentance*, c. iv. § 1.

WITCH. This was not once restrained, as it now is, to the *female* exerciser, of unlawful magical arts, but would have been as freely applied to Balaam or Simon Magus as to her whom we call the 'Witch' of Endor.

There was a man in that citie whose name was Symount, a *wicche*.

Acts viii. 9. Wiclif.

Item he is a *witch*, asking counsel at soothsayers.

Foxe, *The Book of Martyrs; Appeal against Boniface.*

Who can deny him a wisard or *witch*, who in the reign of Richard the Usurper foretold that upon the same stone where he dashed his spur riding toward Bosworth field he should dash his head in his return?

John Cotta, *The Trial of Witchcraft*, p. 49.

WOMB. This is now only the ὑστέρα, but once had as wide a meaning as the κοιλία, of the Greeks.

And he coveitide to fille his *wombe* of the coddis that the hoggis eeten, and no man gaf hym.

Luke xv. 16. Wiclif.

Of this matere, o Poule, well canst thou trete;
Mete unto *wombe*, and *wombe* eke unto mete.

Chaucer, *The Canterbury Tales.*

Falstaff. An I had but a belly of any indifferency, I were simply the most active fellow in Europe. My *womb*, my *womb*, my *womb* undoes me.

Shakespeare, 2 *King Henry IV.*, Act iv. Sc. 3.

WORM. This, which designates at present only the smaller and innoxious kinds of creeping and crawling things, once, as the German 'Wurm' to the present day, was employed of all the serpent kind.

There came a *viper* out of the heat and leapt on his hand. When the men of the country saw the *worm* hang on his hand, they said, This man must needs be a murderer.

Acts xxviii. 3, 4. Tyndale.

'Tis slander,
Whose edge is sharper than the sword; whose tongue
Outvenoms all the *worms* of Nile.

Shakespeare, *Cymbeline*, Act iii. Sc. 4.

O Eve, in evil hour didst thou give ear
To that false *worm*, of whomsoever taught
To counterfeit man's voice.

Milton, *Paradise Lost*, b. ix.

WORSHIP. At present we 'worship' none but God; there was a time when the word was employed in so much more general a sense that it was not profane to say that God 'worshipped,' that is honored, man.

This, of course, was the sense of the word when those words found place in the Marriage Service, "with my body I thee *worship.*"

If ony man serve me, my fadir schal *worschip* hym.

John xii. 26. Wiclif.

That they show all good faithfulness, that they may do *worship* to the doctrine of our Saviour God in all things.

Tit. ii. 10. Tyndale.

Man, that was made after the image and likeness of God, is full worshipful in his kind; yea, this holy image that is man God *worshippeth.*

Foxe, *The Book of Martyrs; Examination of William Thorpe.*

WRETCHED. What has been observed on 'unhappy' explains and accounts also for the use of 'wretched' as = wicked. 'Wretch' still continues to cover the two meanings of one miserable or one wicked, though 'wretched' does so no more.

Nero reigned after this Claudius, of alle men *wrechidhest,* redy to alle maner vices.

Capgrave, *Chronicle of England,* p. 62.

THE END.

www.ingramcontent.com/pod-product-compliance
Lightning Source LLC
LaVergne TN
LVHW050527100826
845148LV00002B/470

* 9 7 8 1 4 2 5 5 1 9 8 4 1 *